Chasing Soap Bubbles

Ecclesiastes

By

David Arnold

Thank you to my wife, Linda, for all her love and care, and for her help and encouragement with my writings. Thank you to my family for their continued support.

Table of Contents

Introduction   7

Chapter 1

  Wisdom and Knowledge   13

Chapter 2

  Wine, Women, and Song   29

Chapter 3

  An Unpredictable World, a

    Predictable God   39

Chapter 4

  The Oppressed, Success,

    Benevolence, Popularity   53

Chapter 5

  Happiness   63

Chapter 6

  The Abundance of Things   77

Chapter 7

Separation and Sorrow   87

Chapter 8

Wisdom   111

Chapter 9

Four Observations   133

Chapter 10

Wise Sayings and Observations   157

Chapter 11

An Exhortation and Admonition   179

Chapter 12

The Whole Duty of Man   197

Conclusion   213

Ecclesiastes

Introduction

Ecclesiastes was written during the latter end of Solomon's reign, and is an account of his apostasy from God (1 Kings 11: 1 – 6). He describes his experiences and the lessons he learned when he was out of fellowship with God. Solomon was a wise man, but he failed to follow his own wisdom. Ecclesiastes has its origin in his tragic sin of forsaking God, and seeking satisfaction in philosophy and science "under the sun." It was a life based on speculation and thought. The message Solomon presents is, apart from God, life is full of misery and emptiness. This is not God's argument, but God's record of man's argument. The whole of life, Solomon declares, is that all things are a puff of wind…transitory, futile, vain. In twelve chapters, he proves this. Solomon does so to lead man to true life, and to the fear of God.

Contrary to some opinions, Ecclesiastes is not a negative view of life, but, instead, an honest one. Some of the Scriptures are sad and pessimistic, but this is because it deals with the grim realities of life. The purpose and message of the book is to teach us the vanity of everything apart from God. It weans us from the love of the world (1 John 2: 15 – 17; Matthew 6: 19 – 21; Colossians 3: 2). It convinces us of the vanity of this world. It proves the insufficiency of the world to makes us happy, the vileness of sin and how it leads to misery, and how comfort and satisfaction are found only in serving God.

Comparing Proverbs and Ecclesiastes

(Both books were written by Solomon.)

Proverbs was written during the early part of his reign when he walked with God. Ecclesiastes was written during the latter part of his reign, when sin had separated him from God.

Proverbs teaches that wisdom has its source in God. Ecclesiastes reveals that merely natural wisdom, apart from God, cannot lead to truth and happiness.

In Proverbs, we can sense joy and contentment that finds its origin in godly wisdom. In Ecclesiastes, we can note a feeling of despair, sadness, and perplexity, as Solomon sees the failure of natural wisdom to solve human problems and bring true happiness. After Solomon drifted from God, he still had his riches and wisdom. Possessing these, he began his search for truth and happiness apart from God. The result was emptiness and worthlessness ("vanity"). Solomon learned that without God's blessings, wisdom, position, and wealth do not satisfy, but only brings disappointment.

Professional and world-renowned tennis star, Boris Becker, when at the top of the tennis world, ironically, was on the brink of suicide. He said, "I had won Wimbledon twice before, once as the youngest player. I was rich. I had all the material possessions I needed. It's the old song of movie stars and pop stars who commit suicide. They have everything, and yet they are so unhappy. I had no inner peace. I was a puppet on a string."[1]

When Solomon speaks of "vanity" in Ecclesiastes, he uses a Hebrew word that is used metaphorically of anything transitory, frail, unsatisfying. It also speaks of a breath of air, or a breeze, to denote emptiness or nothingness, much like a soap bubble. A soap bubble is an extremely thin film of soapy water, enclosing air that forms a hollow sphere with an iridescent surface. Soap bubbles usually last for only a few seconds before bursting, either on their own or from some contact with another object. Soap bubbles are attractive, but to try and grasp them, you discover that they have no lasting substance.

Boris Becker is not the only one to feel a sense of emptiness and lack of fulfillment in worldly gain. History is strewn with those who struggled with the same frustration and disappointment. Jack Higgins, author of the successful novel, *The Eagle Has Landed*, was asked what he would like to have known as a boy. He answered, "That when you get to the top, there's nothing there."[2] Human life, apart from God, even at its best, has no ultimate significance, and, consequently is valueless. It is much like "chasing soap bubbles." This is the lesson the wise man presents in Ecclesiastes.

CHAPTER ONE

"Wisdom and Knowledge"

The Title of the Book
(V. 1)

Solomon calls himself "the preacher." The word for "preacher" in Hebrew is *koheleth*, meaning "convener, to collect together, to gather," and "assemble." It means one who assembles a congregation. The idea is that of being a public speaker in an assembly, hence the word "preacher." This word is found seven times in Ecclesiastes (1: 1, 2, 12; 7: 27; 12: 8 – 10), and four times in the New Testament (Romans 10: 14; 1Timothy 2: 7; 2 Timothy 1: 11; 2 Peter 2: 5).

Nehemiah, admonishing the people of his day about violating the law of God, said of him, "Did not Solomon, King of Israel, sin by these things? Yet among many nations there was no king like him who was beloved of his God; and God made him king over all Israel. Nevertheless, pagan women caused even him to sin," Nehemiah 13:2. So, by calling himself "the Preacher," Solomon could have meant:

1. One who has been gathered from wandering. His love for his wives had caused him to go astray. Now, he sees himself as one gathered back to the fold... as a careless sheep. He had tried "it all," and now he returns to God. The grace of God can make great sinners into great converts (Jeremiah 3: 22). It is only the true repentant who finds forgiveness, the one who is willing to be "gathered to God" (Jeremiah 3: 12-14).

2.	One who is gathering others. He had been "gathered," now, he is doing his utmost to "gather" others who, like him, had gone astray because of his bad example. He that has done anything to seduce his brother ought to do all he can to restore him.

Penitents should be preachers. Those who have heeded the warning to turn and live should warn others not to go on and die. Jesus told Peter, "When you are converted, strengthen your brethren" (Luke 22: 32).

Solomon calls himself "the son of David." Could he, by calling himself this, have felt honored to be the son of such a great man? Could he have meant that it brought more sorrow to him to think of the good education and prayers his father gave him, yet he committed such foolish acts of sin? According to Jeremiah 22: 15 – 17, it aggravated Jehoiakim's sin that he was the son of godly Josiah. Could he have meant that since his father David had sinned, yet found mercy, this was hope to him that he too would find forgiveness? Still others believe that Solomon called himself "the son of David," because he knew that even though God would chasten him for his sin, He would never break his covenant with David's seed (Psalm 89: 34).

Solomon calls himself the "king of Jerusalem." He was a king, and because of his royalty, no king had any business falling into the foolishness Solomon did. According to 1 Peter 2: 9, God's people should refrain from the foolishness of sin, because of who they are!

He was a king, thus, when he preached, his messages should contain more authority in the hearts of the people. Ephesians 4: 11 informs us that, being "gifts" to the Church, they should have authority in their messages.

The Vanity of the World
Stated and Explained
(Vv. 2, 3)

The world is vanity (v. 2). The word "vanity," in the Hebrew, means "emptiness"... that which lacks substance, and, in reality, is like chasing "soap bubbles." "All is vanity," besides God, even the "all" of this world.

The one who said this was not someone who had little experience with life, but one who had "tried it all" (things considered vanity in Ecclesiastes), and found "all" to have no substance or reality!

He lists 30 things as vanity:

1. All things (1: 2, 14; 2: 11, 17; 3: 19)

2. Man's labor under the sun (1: 3)

3. Monotony of all things (1: 8 – 11; 3: 15)

4. All things done under heaven (1: 13 – 14)

5. Wisdom and knowledge (1: 15 – 18)

6. Personal pleasures (2: 1 – 3)

7. Great public and private works (2: 4 – 6)

8. Riches and glory (2: 7 – 9)

9. Unbridled lusts and passions (2: 10, 11)

10. Wisdom, madness, folly (2: 12 – 17)

11. Insecurity of works (2: 18 – 19)

12. Unworthy inheritance (2: 20 – 21)

13. No personal profit from labors (2: 22 – 23)

14. Hard life ending in judgment (2:24 - 26)

15. Weary round of life (3:1-22)

16. Oppression of poor (4:1- 4)

17. Miser's life (4:7-8)

18. No justice or lasting pleasure (4:13-16)

19. Love of money (5:10)

20. Riches saved by others (5:13-17)

21. No power to enjoy blessings of life (6:1-2)

22. Bringing up a large family and dying a pauper (6:3-6)

23. Desires and appetites never satisfied (6:7-9)

24. Continual questions about life (6:10-12)

25. Oppression and sin (8:9-10)

26. Unequal rewards (8:14)

27. Man's ceaseless work (8:16-17)

28. Sameness of life (9:2- 6)

29. Life itself (11:8)

30. Childhood and youth (11:9-10) [1]

The world cannot make man happy (v. 3). Solomon asks here, "What profit has a man from all his labor?" He is saying, "What's the use of living?" This is not the attitude of the true believer in fellowship with God, but rather the attitude of backslidden Solomon. True Old Testament believers did not adopt this attitude. They had a hope for the future. Their trust was in God. Solomon was looking at life from an earthly standpoint. Thus, he saw it as having no goal, just an endless repetition.

The business of this world is labor. The word "labor" signifies toil. The labor of this world constantly wearies and fatigues people. To make this point, he uses the phrase "labor under the sun" twenty-eight times in Ecclesiastes.

There is no real profit from this labor. If we had all the wealth and pleasure of this world, it would not make us happy and fulfilled.

Nothing about the wealth, pleasures, and possessions of this world can satisfy our soul's thirst and hunger. Labor will profit us as far as supplying our earthly, fleshly needs, but it will not satisfy our soul's needs.

The Vanity of the World Proven
(Vv. 4 – 11)

The shortness of life proves it (v. 4). We only live on this earth during our generation. Soon, we will die and make room for the next. All of our worldly possessions we get from others. We will leave them to others, so they are vanity. The earth "abides forever," but we live our life on this earth and pass on. The words "abides forever" come from the Hebrew word *olam*, meaning "time without mind, without any definite limits, eternal, everlasting, perpetual eternity, forever and ever." The word is used seven times (1:4, 10:2:26; 3:11, 14; 9:6; 12:5). See also James 4:14.

The revolution of nature proves it (Vv. 5 – 7). This is the weary round of nature. When the sun rises, it hastens to set, then hastens to rise (v. 5). The winds are always shifting (v. 6). The waters are in continual circulation (v. 7). The thought is that life does not seem to be going anywhere. It is a ceaseless round, and, in nature, it is most obvious. The question is, "Is life really going anywhere? Is there any profit in it after all?"

The lack of satisfaction proves it (v. 8). Everyone is so busy being preoccupied with their labor, that they have no time to show an interest in others. The eye and ear continually see and hear the same thing, and cannot be satisfied.

The lack of nothing new proves it (Vv. 9, 10). There is nothing really new. In some way, either directly or indirectly, it has all been done, said, and thought before.

The lack of memory proves it (v. 11). Many think that through certain accomplishments they will always be remembered. There have been many who were very great, renowned, and noble in their day, but now are buried in oblivion.

Psalm 49: 11, 12

The Vanity of Man's Knowledge
(Vv. 12 – 18)

Through knowledge, Solomon sought to find happiness. Nothing could be a closed book to him. He wanted to know everything. He wanted to be the world's wisest man, the most knowledgeable, the most cultured. With all his goals, he found that "in much wisdom is much grief, and he that increases knowledge increases sorrow" (v. 18).

Solomon sought for knowledge (Vv. 12, 13, 14a, 16, 17). His position as king allowed him to seek for knowledge (v. 12). He had his throne in Jerusalem, which was then the eye of the world. Because he was king, it was only natural that he search out wisdom. As king, he had access to knowledge that few would have. He applied himself to seeking knowledge (v. 13). Solomon gave his "heart to seek and search" for wisdom and knowledge.

He lists eight things he gave his heart to search after:

1. He gave his heart to know madness and folly (1:17).

2. He gave his heart to mirth and pleasure (1: 17– 21).

3. He gave his heart to wine and drunkenness (2: 3).

4. He gave his heart to folly (2: 3).

5. He set his heart on riches, treasures, singing, music, and all that is connected with such a life (2: 8).

6. He gave himself over to unbridled lust and passions (2: 10).

7. He applied his heart to know the wickedness of folly and the foolishness of madness (7: 25).

8. He had bitter experiences with women (1 Kings 11: 1 – 10) [2]

He wanted to discover "all things that are done under heaven." He set out to discover all things about man, animals, mathematics, philosophy, history, etc. – all that is under heaven!

His use of the word "God" is interesting. This is not the word "Jehovah," the covenant name of the God of Israel. He never uses the name "Jehovah" once in Ecclesiastes, though he used the name of God 40 times. This is an indication of his backslidden condition. Before this, he often used the name Jehovah and God. In 1 Kings 1 – 11 and 2 Chronicles 1 – 9, the name of God, other than Elohim, occurs 197 times. His abstaining from the use of Jehovah is no oversight on his part. He purposely did this, because he did not consider himself in a covenant relationship with God. The name "God" in 1:13 refers to God as creator, and worker in relationship with his creatures.

He progressed tremendously in knowledge (v. 14a – "I have seen all the works that are done under the sun"). He diligently applied himself, and succeeded in gaining extraordinary knowledge and wisdom. He was a very studious man, and, for this, he is to be commended. It is proper to be studious and to apply oneself to gaining knowledge, but to depend upon this to satisfy the cravings of the soul is "vexation of spirit" ("a grasping for the wind").

Solomon saw the vanity of such knowledge (v. 14b – "And indeed, all is vanity and grasping for the wind"). It is futile. It is like chasing the wind.

Solomon saw the limits of knowledge (v. 15). He is saying that, no matter how much knowledge he acquired, there was always something that eluded him.

He used his knowledge to gain wisdom (Vv. 16, 17). He studied wise men, mad men, and men of folly. The word "madness" means "to make a show, to boast, to be clamorously foolish, to rave, to celebrate, to show or display loss of self-control, to rave with self-conceit." The word "folly" means "silliness." This is his conclusion of such endeavors and opinion of such people.

He saw the lack of satisfaction in knowledge (v. 18). There is much pain in getting it, and a great deal of effort to remember it. He concludes "in much wisdom is much grief." This is true when a wise person gives himself over to madness and folly. Their bragging, vainness, and self-display will bring them to grief, because people will reject them. Lesson: In humility, gain wisdom and knowledge, always remembering the true source – God! (James 1:5)

"Wine, Women, and Song"

In chapter one, Solomon shows the vanity of trying to gain soul satisfaction through wisdom and knowledge. In chapter two, he shows the vanity of pleasure… "wine, women, and song." He tells how he built himself houses and fancy gardens, a large staff, collected valuable antiques, and became Jerusalem's richest man. Whatever he wanted, he took. Then he says, "This is also vanity and grasping for the wind" (2: 26).

Joy, Pleasure, and the Gratification of the Flesh

(Vv. 1 – 11)

Here, Solomon leaves his study chamber where he sought satisfaction through intellectual increase, and journeys to the playground of mirth and pleasure. Just as there are those who have mistakenly thought spiritual satisfaction could be found in much wisdom and knowledge, so there are those who believe satisfaction is found in joy, pleasure, and fleshly gratification.

He tried entertainment (Vv. 1, 2). Solomon says that he thought he would be satisfied if he could constantly entertain himself with much stories, jesting, and frivolity; if he could constantly be with the "in crowd."

He experimented with it (v. 1a). Having already discovered that "in much wisdom is much grief," he decided to make himself "jovial and happy." He wrote, "I said in my heart." No godly person would say such a thing in his heart, so this is more proof that he has "wandered away from the fold." The word "mirth" means "joy" and "pleasure," and speaks of any festivity or pleasure that satisfies the lusts and passions of the flesh momentarily.

He saw the vanity of it, declaring, "But surely, this is also vanity," like all the rest, because it brings no true fulfillment (v. 1b). He warns, "I said of laughter, 'It is madness;' and of mirth, 'What does it accomplish?'" (v. 2). Joy, laughter, parties, etc., are good in moderation, and are very helpful in relieving the tensions of life, but excessiveness is foolish and fruitless. It does little lasting good, will not relieve a guilty conscience, ease a broken heart, and will never satisfy the soul. Nothing is more ungrateful than singing songs to a heavy heart. It is only a deceitful cure for grief. Great laughter and frivolity commonly end with a sigh. Further, it causes hurt, for "it is madness." It causes people to act in ways, and do things that later bring shame and embarrassment. It draws people away from being serious with God.

Sir William Temple said, "Laughter and pleasure come from very different affections of the mind; for, as men have no disposition to laugh at things they are most pleased with, so they are very little pleased with many things they laugh at."[1]

He tried the gratification of flesh (v. 3). He only tried this after he had sought satisfaction in wisdom and knowledge. Until the increase of wisdom brought an increase of sorrow, he never thought of giving himself over to wine. Sadly, instead of turning to God, he turned to wine. He looked upon this as folly, "I searched in my heart how to gratify my flesh with wine" (v. 3a). He took care to continue in wisdom that he might govern himself in the gratification of the flesh, "while guiding my heart with wisdom, and how to lay hold on folly" (v. 3b). He thought he could experience both wisdom and wine. He discovered, though, this was as useless as trying to serve God and mammon, for "wine is a mocker, strong drink is raging, and whosoever is deceived thereby is not wise" (Proverbs 20: 1). He gave himself to gratifying his flesh to see if this would bring happiness... "till I might see what was good for the sons of men to do under heaven all the days of their lives" (v. 3c).

He tried pleasure (Vv. 4 – 11). This included much building (v. 4) (1 Kings 9: 15 – 19), gardening (v. 5), and public works, such as paradises, parks, pleasure grounds, all kinds of fruit trees, and many pools of water (v. 6).[2] He increased his family (Ezra 2: 58 – "All the Nethinim and the children of Solomon's servants were three hundred ninety and two"). He tried ranching (v. 7). He grew very rich (1 Kings 10: 27 – "And the king (Solomon) made silver to be in Jerusalem as stones"), then had the money to try all kinds of music (v. 8).

He tried more than all others before him (Vv. 9 – 11). Even though the wisdom God gave him was in his head, he still failed to be guided by it (v. 9), and he confessed that wise people do foolish things if they do not listen to their own wisdom. His wisdom served as no restrainer to his pleasure (v. 10). He fulfilled every lust and passion that his heart craved. This is the result of shutting one's ear to wisdom. He passed judgment on it all (v. 11). "All his unbridled lusts proved to be nothing but vanity when they were fulfilled. There was nothing Solomon desired which he could not have; and there was nothing that he could have that he did not experience or possess; yet nothing satisfied him. Everything left him empty and feeling that all was vain, thus it will always be with the man who turns from God after having known Him and been fully satisfied with His (God's) blessings"[3] (2 Peter 2: 20 – 22).

He Compares Wisdom and Folly
(Vv. 12 – 16)

He considered both wisdom and folly (v. 12). He says he has studied all subjects, folly and pleasure, and experimented with these things more than any other man, giving preference to wisdom (Vv. 13, 14). He then admits that even wisdom cannot satisfy the desires of the soul, because both the wise and the fool fair alike, and both are forgotten as much as the other (Vv. 15, 16).

"Three discoveries of Solomon: 1. That there is no supreme good or lasting happiness in all pursuits of science, no genuine satisfaction in unbridled lusts, no true joy in folly, and that wisdom excels folly as much as light excels darkness (v. 13). 2. That the wise man's eyes are in his head and he weighs carefully the consequences of all he does, whereas the fool has no guide to his reason and no check on his passions as he blindly walks, groping in unbridled lusts (v. 14). 3. That both the wise man and the fool die and that there is no more remembrance of a wise man than a fool forever (Vv. 15 16)."[4]

He Sees the Vanity of Business and the Wealth of This World
(Vv. 17 – 26)

He refers to it as "the work done under the sun" (Vv. 17-23). He says "Therefore I hated life," because it seemed to be so useless with no real purpose or accomplishment (v. 17). He hated all his labor, because he knew he would leave it all behind when he died. Those whom he left it to, he would not know if they were fools or wise (Vv. 18-19). Not only did he hate life and labor, but he despaired to think that what he had acquired through hard work would be left to unworthy people. This bothered him night and day (Vv. 20-23).

He concluded that the best thing is to enjoy the wealth one has (Vv. 24 – 26). There is good in wealth, so wealth is to be enjoyed (Vv. 24, 25). A person should be content with and enjoy what God has blessed them with, while using what God has blessed them with to support the work of God, remembering that it is from the hand of God (v. 26a) (Deuteronomy 8: 18).

What is the result of all this search? Again Solomon experienced emptiness, going in the wrong direction, away from God, "This is also vanity and grasping for the wind" (v. 26b).

CHAPTER THREE

"An Unpredictable World, a Predictable God"

Solomon was "a poor rich man." He was surrounded by luxury to the utmost degree. He left nothing out of his life that he thought could make him happy. Yet he only found emptiness even after experiencing the best the world had to offer. The life he lived made both his present and future depressing. He finally came to the conclusion that man is no better than an animal, and in one sense, he was correct. If a man lives only for himself and the present, leaving God out of his life, he is no better off than an animal. In fact, he is worse off, for an animal's death means the end. However, a man's death means that he must face God and give an account for his life.

Solomon here shows we live in a world of constant change, because the world goes from one extreme to the other. However, every change in this world is under the control of an Almighty God. This should cause us to trust God as He directs this world. We should never "set our affections on the earth" that is constantly changing, but "on things above," where God is, who never changes, and is always dependable.

"Life is Constantly Changing"
(Vv. 1 – 10)

He tells what he has learned (v. 1). Everything in this world is in constant revolution, "To everything there is a season" (v. 1a). Darkness replaces light, poverty replaces plenty, emptiness replaces fullness, winter replaces summer, and joy replaces sorrow. Everything in this world is determined by the foreknowledge of God, "A time for every purpose under heaven" (v. 1b). Daniel 2: 20 – 22, "Blessed be the name of God forever and ever, for wisdom and might are His. And He changes the times and the seasons; He removes kings and raises up kings; He gives wisdom to the wise and knowledge to those who have understanding. He reveals deep and secret things; He knows what is in the darkness, and light dwells with Him."

He proves what he has learned (Vv. 2 – 8). There is a time to be born and a time to die, "A time to be born, and a time to die" (v. 2a). Man's birth is determined by the foreknowledge of our all-wise God (Ephesians 1:4). Man's death is determined by the foreknowledge of our all-wise God (Hebrews 9: 27; Acts 17: 24 – 28).

There is a time to plant and a time to reap, "A time to plant, and a time to pluck what is planted" (v. 2b) . In John 4:34-38, Christ said the time is now for us to plant and reap. Psalm 126: 5, 6, "Those who sow in tears (plant), will reap in joy (harvest). He who continually goes forth weeping, bearing seed (planting) for sowing, will doubtless come again with rejoicing, bringing his sheaves with him (harvesting)."

There is a time for judgment and a time for mercy, "A time to kill and a time to heal" (v. 3). God's judgment must come at times. God's healing mercy must also come. Hosea 6: 1-3. "Come, and let us return to the Lord; for He has torn, but He will heal us; He has stricken, but He will bind us up. After two days He will revive us; on the third day He will raise us up, that we may live in His sight. Let us know, let us pursue the knowledge of the Lord. His going forth is established as the morning; He will come to us like the rain, like the latter and the former rain to the earth."

There is a time to break down and a time to build up, "A time to break down, and a time to build up" (v. 3b). Some things must come to an end to make way for the new. Some things must be rebuilt, or built for the first time (Psalm 102: 13, 16).

There is a time to weep, laugh, mourn, and dance (v. 4). There are times when the best thing to do is to weep and mourn, such as during death and calamity. There are times when the best thing to do is to laugh and dance, such as times of God's blessings, prosperity, health and healing, etc.

There is a time to plan and prepare, "A time to cast away stones, and a time to gather stones" (v. 5a). This seems to be referring to the job of clearing a vineyard of stones, as mentioned in Isaiah 5:2, and of collecting materials for making structures, such as fences, wine-press towers, etc., and of repairing roads.

There is a time to embrace and to refrain from embracing, "A time to embrace and a time to refrain from embracing" (v. 5b). There are times to show love and affection to a faithful friend. There are times to withdraw from those who have proven to be unfaithful.

There is a time to get and to lose, "A time to gain and a time to lose" (v. 6a). Throughout life, there will be losses and gains, and one should accept this as sometimes an inevitable event, being flexible.

There is a time to be prudent, "A time to keep and a time to throw away" (v. 6b). It is wise sometimes to deprive oneself of some things in order to gain more important things, as when sailors throw cargo overboard to save their ship and their lives. It can also apply to self-denial for the purpose of greater gains. Further, there are things we should keep, as long as they do not hinder our walk with God. There are things that must be cast away if they become a spiritual hindrance (Matthew 5: 29, 30).

There is a time to repent and return, "A time to tear and a time to sew" (v. 7a). There is a time to rend our hearts in repentance, and a time to "sew" – return and do our first works (Joel 2: 13, 14; Revelation 2: 5).

There is a time to guard our tongue, "A time to keep silent and a time to speak" (v. 7b). There is a time for sympathizing silence, a time for wise counsel, and a time to only speak about things we are knowledgeable of (Proverbs 17:27 – 28).

There is a time to love and a time to hate, "A

time to love and a time to hate" (v. 8a). We should love God, His people, our fellow man, etc. We should hate Satan, sin, injustice, etc.

There is a time for war and for peace (v. 8b – "a time of war and a time of peace." There is a time to go to war, when there is no alternative. There is a time to make and keep peace, when at all possible.

He tells of his conclusion (Vv. 9, 10). All our effort in life is ultimately vain. Everything we work and toil for on this earth will be broken down or passed on to others (v. 9). If we make proper use of this earth, with eternity in view, we will profit from it (v. 10). God never gave us this earth to make us happy in it. We are spiritual beings, and nothing of this world can satisfy us. We are made for much higher things. God allows us to be stewards of earthly things. He expects us to be faithful with what we have here, and not set our heart on them, so He can prepare us to be trusted with the eternal (Matthew 25: 21 Luke 16: 9–12).

The Hand of God is in All of Life
(Vv. 11–15)

This should make us content with God's providential care, "He has made everything beautiful in its time" (v. 11a). Everything in this world is under His watchful care. No matter how bleak or depressing things are, they are serving the purposes of God. All events are related, no matter how separated by distance or time, and will all come together as God has determined (Romans 8:28; Ephesians 1: 9, 10).

This should make us content with our understanding of things, "Also he has put eternity in their hearts, except that no one can find out the work that God does from beginning to end" (v. 11b). We do not understand all things that happen, both good and bad, thus we are incompetent judges to decide what is right or wrong. We only see a small portion of the purposes of God at work. We did not see the beginning, and we probably will not see all the ending. It is much like the work of an architect and builder. We see the building on paper, and then the frame is built. To the untrained eye it is confusing. However, if we will continue watching, we will see that a beautiful building is the result. (Isaiah 55: 8 – 11; 1 Corinthians 2: 9 – 16)

This should make us content with the will of God for our lives in this world (Vv. 12, 13). It will benefit others (v. 12)… we were not born for ourselves, but for others. We are our brother's keeper, and we should be faithful where God has placed us to bless others (1 Corinthians 12: 24 – 2). It will benefit us (v. 13). There is nothing greater than to realize that life itself is a gift from God, and He has given us all things to enjoy.

This should cause us to be satisfied with the way God has established things (Vv. 14, 15). God's purposes cannot be altered, "I know that whatever God does, it shall be forever" (v. 14a). Job 23: 13, "But He is of one mind, and who can turn Him? And what His soul desires, even that He does." This does not mean that God has purposed the eternal destiny of a soul. People are free, moral, intelligent individuals. Nowhere does Scripture teach God has purposed the destiny of a soul. If we yield to Him, we receive reward. If we rebel, we receive judgment. God's purposes are perfect, "Nothing can be added to it and nothing taken from it" (v. 14b). If we could see the whole counsel of God, we would see a perfect work. Psalm 18:30, "As for God, His way is perfect." This should cause us to turn our heart to God, "God does it, that men should fear before him" (v. 14c). All the ways, purposes, and counsels of God are for turning men to Him. This should cause us to trust His faithfulness (v. 15). God is not "new" at this. His purposes were established in eternity past and have always been.

The Vanity of Worldly Power and Honor

(Vv. 16 – 22)

Even a powerful man is vanity (Vv. 16, 17). He will abuse his power (v. 16a), doing more harm than good with it (v. 16b), and will one day be judged (v. 17). Hebrews 9:27, "...it is appointed unto men once to die, but after this the judgment."

A man without God is vanity (Vv. 18 – 22). He tells why this is so (v. 18). God will be honored, "I said in my heart, 'concerning the condition of the sons of men'" (v. 18a). He is saying that God has done all He can to give a man a meaningful life. If that man has a miserable one, it is his own fault. God cannot be blamed. Man may be humbled, "God tests them that they may see that they themselves are like animals" (v. 18b). People will have no better purpose in life than an animal, if they do not serve God.

He proves how this is so (Vv. 19 – 21). What happens to men without God happens to beasts, "For what happens to the sons of men also happens to animals" (v. 19a). When the judgment of God comes, as in Noah's day, it falls on man and beast alike. They both end the same way (Vv. 19b -21). They both have breath, "One thing befalls them: as one dies, so dies the other. Surely, they all have one breath; man has no advantage over beasts, for all is vanity" (v. 19b). They both return to dust (v. 20). The beasts perish at death, but so does the soul of the unsaved (v. 21). The beasts perish in the sense that they return to a condition as though they had never existed. The soul of the unsaved perishes in the sense that they are lost forever without God.

He expresses his conclusion (v. 22). This is the conclusion of a backslidden man. He is saying, "The best thing to do is to enjoy life." This is not true! The best thing is to live a life unto God (Acts 17: 28).

CHAPTER FOUR

"The Oppressed, Success, Benevolence, and Popularity"

"The Oppressed"
(Vv. 1 – 3)

According to 1 Kings 4: 29, Solomon had a compassionate heart for the less fortunate. Here, in these first three verses, he writes about them.

He describes their troubles (v. 1). Laborers are oppressed by their employers. Children are oppressed and mistreated by their parents. The wealthy oppress and manipulate the poor.

He describes their condition (Vv. 2, 3). They are tempted to hate and despise life because of their condition. They actually envy those who are dead in the grave, and wish they had never been born. Solomon tends to agree with them. He says the dead are better off (v. 2). Those who know the Lord and have it "rough" in life, if it be God's will, are better off dead. They have gone on to their reward. He says those who have never been born are the happiest (v. 3). He declares that it is better to have never been born if all one is going to see is the world's troubles and evils. This is not true, though, of those who are living, for they are alive on this earth in the providence of God. The reason Solomon says it is better to have never been born is because he was writing this from a backslidden and miserable condition.

"Success"

(Vv. 4 – 6)

Solomon says to strive for success is vanity. It is not "success" itself, but to think "success" is your panacea is what leads to disappointment.

Success creates jealousy (v. 4).The neighbors will be jealous of the successful man. Even though he "toils," that is, he works diligently, and is wise and prudent, and sacrifices to reach success, his neighbors will still be jealous. Even though he accomplishes success through "every skillful work," that is, he is totally honest and defrauds no one, he is still envied. Jealousy is a price a man must pay for success. No matter how wise and good a successful man is, there are always those who are jealous of him. Those who are industrious will always be envied by the undisciplined and slothful. This should cause the prudent, hardworking man to seek to please

God, realizing he will never please man. You cannot please God, and please everyone else at the same time!

Jealousy is foolish (v. 5). The jealous man in verse 4 is a foolish man in verse 5, because he destroys himself. Jealousy will cause a man to be slothful, and this will only lead to failure. Jealousy will cause a man to be just the opposite of the industrious man of whom he is jealous. The slothful, jealous man is only ruining himself (Proverbs 12: 24; Proverbs 18: 9; Proverbs 19: 24; Proverbs 21: 25; Proverbs 26: 13; Proverbs 19: 15; Ecclesiastes 10: 18; Romans 12: 11). Idleness is a sin that is its own punishment.

Moderation is wise (v. 6). It is better to be content with your needs met than to be constantly concerned over abundance 1 Timothy 6: 6 – 10).

"Benevolence"
(Vv. 7 – 12)

It is foolish to collect wealth, and not put it to beneficial use. The danger with abundance is that the more a person has, the more they want; they never take time to enjoy what they do have.

Selfishness causes materialistic foolishness (Vv. 7, 8). The problem with abundance is that it can become an end in itself, blinding a person to the real purposes of life. It causes selfishness; (v. 7) Solomon explains how a miser's life is one of extreme loneliness and dissatisfaction in the midst of plenty.

A person becomes a slave to business, "There is one alone, without companion; he has neither son nor brother. Yet there is no end to all his labors" (v.8a). He has no one for compassionate. He does not marry and have a family, because he doesn't want the expense of one. He works night and day only to accumulate more for himself (Psalm 127:2). He has no one else he is obligated to; he has no one to leave it to.

He never thinks he has enough, "Nor is his eye satisfied with riches" (v. 8b). This is covetousness which is described as "the lust of the eye" (1 John 2: 16). In chapter 5, verse 11, we are told how he accumulates wealth so he can look at it, and know that he has it. He has enough for his "back and belly," but not enough for his "eyes."

He cannot enjoy what he has… "But he never asks, 'For whom do I toil and deprive myself of good?'" (v. 8c) He misses the true meaning of life because of his covetousness.

A person cannot see his error… "this also is vanity and a grave misfortune" (v. 8d). He fails to see that he is not laboring for God's glory. He fails to see that he is laboring for a physical body that will one day return to dust. He fails to see that fools will inherit what he has worked so hard to acquire. If a person fails to consider the goal of all their labor, then their labor is vanity.

Liberality brings materialistic freedom (Vv. 9 – 12). Solomon establishes the truth of it, "Two are better than one, because they have a good reward for their labor" (v. 9). By sharing, two are blessed and made happy, and not just one.

Solomon proves the truth of it (Vv. 10 – 12). Liberality brings help in emergencies (v. 10). If one gets into trouble, there is the other to help him. However, the one who "goes it alone" has no one in time of distress. Liberality brings friendship (v. 11). The man who is liberal has a friend to encourage and minister to him in times of need. He enjoys "mutual care." Liberality brings strength (v. 12). If an enemy attacks, the two together can conquer; by themselves, they would both be conquered. The two can add a third friend and their strength is "not quickly broken" (Romans 12: 13 – 21). In Matthew 18: 15 – 20, Christ said that unity brings unlimited power in prayer (a three-fold cord – two unified believers and Christ).

"Popularity"
(Vv. 13 – 16)

Solomon says great position is vanity. He was a great king, so if anyone knew the vanity of position, he did. Proverbs 27: 24, "For riches are not forever, nor does a crown endure to all generations."

He says a person in high position will not be happy unless they have wisdom (Vv. 13, 14). A poor wise child is better off than a foolish old king (v. 13). The poor, wise child has the opportunity to become wise, and prepare himself to be a blessing to his generation. A foolish old king will not have the respect of his subordinates. A poor, wise child can gain position, but a foolish, old king will lose it (v. 14). As Joseph, a poor child who will commit himself to gaining wisdom can be exalted (Psalm 113: 7, 8). No matter if he is "born in his kingdom," if he does not apply himself, the old king will lose his throne. Remember: wisdom and virtue will gain men honor, even under the disadvantage of youth and poverty.

A person in position will not be happy unless he has the following and the confidence of the people (Vv. 15, 16). People always favor the one rising to power, "I saw all the living who walk under the sun; they were with the second youth" (v. 15a). The person in power will live to see someone younger gain the people's confidence and remove them from power, "Who stands in his place" (v. 15b).

People are only temporarily content and satisfied, "There was no end of all the people over whom he was made king" (v. 16a). People have always been this way, "Yet those who come afterward will not rejoice in him" (v. 16b). This breaks the heart of those in power, "Surely this also is vanity and grasping for the wind" (v. 16c).

CHAPTER FIVE

"Happiness"

In this chapter, Solomon says that happiness can only be obtained by a total commitment to and worship of God, by refraining from injustice, greed, and violence, and by being temperate in the enjoyments of life.

Worship God and Devote to Him
(Vv. 1 – 8)

The Scriptures here seek to lead us from the deceitfulness of this world (which always promises, looks delightful and satisfying, but always is disappointing) to a true, deep, meaningful relationship with God. We also see here the vanity of some religious exercises that can easily become substitutes for God!

Solomon gives us five ways to worship God. First, we are to worship God by hearing His word and offering sacrifices (v. 1). By hearing the word, "Walk prudently when you go to the house of God; and draw near to hear" (v. 1a). Go to the house of God to hear the word of God. We are to go to the "assembly of the saints." The more we "assemble together," the more we see the vanity of this world. We need to follow the psalmist's example in Psalm 73:17. He understood certain things after he went to the house of God. Solomon may have regretted his indulgence in the world, but never did he regret his going to the house of God. We should be attentive to the word ("walk prudently...and draw near to hear"). We are to not let our minds wander. We are to discipline our minds to be attentive (Matthew 13: 14 – 18). In Luke 8:18 Jesus said, "Take heed therefore how you hear."

"Walk prudently" is a normal way in Hebrew to tell one to be on his guard. We cannot be careless in the house of God. The word "hear" in Hebrew is often used with the sense of "obey." The truth is that religious talk and ritual that is not consistent with a person's conduct is dangerous. It is the "sacrifice of fools." It is also noteworthy that in the Old Testament, being religious is never looked upon as helpful in itself. It was considered to be a hindrance or dangerous. Religious conduct with a wrong spirit complicates rather than helps a person's relationship with God.

By offering sacrifices, "Rather than to give the sacrifice of fools, for they do not know that they do evil" (v. 1b). Don't offer a fool's sacrifice.

Proverbs 15 : 8 warns that when the wicked (fools) offer sacrifices, it "is an abomination to the Lord." Malachi 1: 8 says that to offer "the blind," "the lame and sick" (i.e., second, third, fourth best) to the Lord is a fool's sacrifice. A person who does this… "do not know that they do evil." They think they are doing themselves and God a good service, but, in reality, they are offending God (Revelation 3: 16, 17). Know what you are doing when you offer a sacrifice. This comes by being attentive to the word of God to know the will of God. This enables us to comply with the will of God as it is made known to us. Only by hearing the word can we offer acceptable sacrifices to God.

Second, we are to worship God by prayer (Vv. 2, 3). Be cautious and considerate as we approach God, "Do not be rash with your mouth and let not your heart utter anything hastily before God" (v. 2a). We are cautioned about what we say, so as not to be "rash," nor "hasty" in our speech. What we say to God must come from our heart. We should never let our tongue out-run our thoughts (Matthew 15: 8, 9).

"Lip-labor, though ever so well-labored, if that be all, is but lost labor in religion. It is not enough that what we say comes from the heart, but it must come from a composed heart, and not from a sudden heat or passion. As the mouth must not be rash, so the heart must not be hasty; we must not only think, but think twice before we speak, when we are to speak either from God in preaching or to God in prayer, and not utter anything indecent and undigested."[1]

Be cautious and considerate in our words to God (Vv. 2b, c, 3). We must never talk to God the way we loosely speak to each other at times.

There is infinite distance between us and God... "for God is in heaven, and you on earth" (v. 2b). He is in Heaven where He rules supreme and sovereign over all. We are on earth, His footstool. This demands that we speak respectful and humble words to Him as we would to a man of great power and renown (Job 9: 14). Also, much speaking makes fools out of us (Vv. 2c, 3).

Much speaking to God in foolish words shows a careless and undisciplined spirit before Him. Only fools think they are heard for their much speaking. Ecclesiastes 10: 11 – 14 says that those that know the least talk the most. This does not mean that long prayers are wrong. Jesus spent all night in prayer (Luke 6: 12); we are told to "continue in prayer" (Colossians 4: 2), and to "pray without ceasing" (1 Thessalonians 5: 17). However, careless, heartless praying ("vain repetitions") is condemned (Matthew 6: 7). The best way to speak to and of God is to speak those words that Scripture speaks.

Third, we are to worship God by vows (Vv. 4 – 6). A vow is a bond upon the soul (v. 4a, c). A vow is something we promise to do either from direct command of God, or of our own free-will. We must pay our vows as "vowed"... "pay what you have vowed" (v. 4c). We must pay the vow exactly as we vowed we would. We must "not alter it, nor change it, a good for a bad, or a bad for a good." Leviticus 27: 10 teaches that we must not delay to pay our vows. "When you make a vow to God, do not delay to pay it" (v. 4a). If we can pay it today, don't delay until tomorrow or a more convenient time. By delaying, the sense of obligation slackens and cools, and is in danger of wearing off. The longer it is put off, the more difficult it will be to pay it.

There are two reasons why we must quickly and cheerfully pay our vows (Vv. 4b, 5). We insult God if we do not, "For He has no pleasure in fools" (v. 4b). Actually, the meaning is "He greatly abhors such fools and such foolish dealings." We lose the blessing of keeping the vow, and bring the curse of breaking it (v. 5). It would have been better to have never vowed the vow. To vow a vow and to break it is lying to God (Acts 5: 4).

We must be cautious in making vows (v. 6). To be cautious makes us conscientious in performing them.

Never should we make a vow that would cause us to sin, "Do not let your mouth cause your flesh to sin" (v. 6a). We must never vow a vow that we are unable to keep (v. 6b, c), for we only bring shame on ourselves, "Nor say before the messenger of God that it was an error"

(v. 6b). The word "angel" is the Hebrew word for "messenger." It is used in Malachi 2:7 of the priest, and may refer here to the priest whose business it was to collect the thing vowed. The thought is that you will embarrass yourself by admitting your foolishness. We expose ourselves to the wrath of God, "Why should God be angry at your excuse and destroy the work of your hands?" (v. 6c) God becomes angry when people vow to Him, then violate that vow. He will destroy their plans and purposes to bring them to repentance. (See Proverbs 20: 25, The Living Bible.)

Fourth, we are to worship God by fearing Him (v. 7). Dreams and many words can lead people away from the fear of God, "For in the multitude of dreams and many words there is also vanity" (v. 7a). People who carelessly heed dreams will become unduly dependent on them. God can speak to His people through dreams, but many dreams are like many words, "vanities," and must be "tested" according to Scripture. In Jeremiah 23: 25, 26, the prophets pretended to know the mind of God by dreams, and make God's people forget His name by their dreams. Fearing God is the answer, "But Fear God" (v. 7b). Reverence Him, set our heart upon knowing Him through His word, and realize that He is the One to be worshiped.

Fifth, we are to worship God by looking to Him (v. 8). It will keep us from depression, "If you see the oppression of the poor and the violent perversion of justice and righteousness in a province, do not marvel at the matter" (v. 8a). The word "marvel" means "to be astounded, dumbfounded, bewildered." If we allow ourselves to, we can become confused over all the oppression, suffering, injustice, etc., in the world. By looking to God, we are kept from getting depressed. It will encourage our trust in God (Vv. 8b, c). We will see that no matter how powerful the oppressors in the world are, God is over them in power and authority... "for high official watches over high official" (v. 8b). We will see that God knows about all these enigmas of life. He sees and observes what is happening. He keeps record of it all to recall it on Judgment Day. Job 21: 23b, "His eyes are upon their ways" (Matthew 10: 29 – 31). We will see that God's angels are protecting people who are being harmed, "And higher officials are over them" (v. 8c). Angels are God's ministers sent to help people.

The World's Wealth is Vanity
(Vv. 9 – 20)

Solomon, speaking from experience, disproves the belief that if a person can just have enough money, he will be happy.

Wealth alone will not satisfy (Vv. 9, 10). The person who loves money and sets his heart upon it, never thinks he has enough. The love for money is a corrupt desire that cannot be satisfied. "Nature is content with little, grace with less, but lust with nothing."

Wealth is unprofitable (v. 11). The more wealth a person obtains, the greater the financial obligations, thus more money is needed to meet those obligations. It becomes a vicious cycle!

Wealth is worrisome (v. 12). The laboring man has peace and contentment. The wealthy man cannot find rest because his lust for abundance robs him of sleep. People desire wealth then find that it does not satisfy when it is gained. The more wealth they accrue, the more financial demands on them. About the only satisfaction a person receives from having wealth is knowing they have it. Wealth brings burdens, and tends to rob a person of values that money cannot buy – peace of heart and mind.

Wealth can become hurtful and destructive (v. 13). Riches make people proud and secure, and draws them away from God and from entering into the kingdom of heaven. Matthew 19: 24 – Riches prevent people from entering into the fullness (joy, peace, righteousness) of God's kingdom (Romans 14: 17). Their riches make them covetous, and prevents them from sharing with the poor. Their riches cause them to worry about the danger of being robbed or losing it. If they did not have wealth, they would not have this worry.

Wealth is perishable (v. 14). The very investments that give a person wealth may take it away from him. A person believes they can leave their wealth to their son, but often at their death, the estate is so in debt that nothing is left to the heir.

Wealth will be left behind at death (Vv. 15, 16). As a person came from their mother's womb naked, so will they go to the grave.

Wealth makes a person uncomfortable when they worship it (v. 17). He "eats in darkness," i.e., he always worries and fears over what he has. He worries himself sick, then frets over the security of his riches while he is sick..."He has much sorrow and sickness and anger."

Wealth is to be used wisely (Vv. 18 – 20). We are to enjoy and be content with what God has given us (v. 18). God has given us wisdom to enjoy His blessings (v. 19). We give ourselves a good life if we do this (v. 20).

"The Abundance of Things"

This chapter shows that happiness does not consist in an abundance of things. For if a person does not use the wealth God has given him for God's glory, then it is all in vain.

The Vanity of Worldly Wealth
(Vv. 1 – 10)

It is a common thing for a person to misuse God's blessings (v. 1). The warning of Psalm 62:10, "If riches increase, do not set your heart on them," is mostly disregarded.

The enjoyments wealth brings to some (Vv.

2a, b, 3a, b, 6a) God gives them abundance… "A man to whom God has given riches wealth and honor" (v. 2a). God gives them all they would ever want, "So that he lacks nothing for himself of all he desires" (v. 2b). This is all due to the goodness of God. Psalm 73: 7, "Their eyes bulge with abundance; they have more than heart could wish." Instead of desiring more of God though, they desire more "things." Psalm 17: 14, "They have their portion in this life." God gives them a large family, "If a man begets a hundred children" (v. 3a). God gives them a long life, "And lives many years so that the days of his years are many" (v. 3b); "Even if he lives a thousand years twice" (v. 6a). God gives them a long life so they might see the vanity of life itself by living such a long life.

Some abuse their wealth (Vv. 2c, d, 3c, d, 6b). Instead of serving the Lord as their source, they abuse what God has blessed them with. Covetousness prevents them from enjoying it, "Yet God does not give him power to eat of it" (v. 2c). They have all that a person would want materially, yet their greed prevents them from enjoying it. Because they are greedy, God will not allow them to enjoy it. Because they will not serve God with it, God denies them the power to serve themselves with it.

Strangers swindle it from them, "But a foreigner consumes it" (v. 2d). This is a common fault of the covetous. They will not trust God or God's people with it, yet they will put it into the hands of strangers for investing. These strangers will attempt to swindle it from them, because they are greedy themselves. Hosea 7: 9, "Strangers have devoured his strength, and he knows it not" (Proverbs 5: 10).

They cannot find satisfaction with it, "But his soul is not satisfied with goodness" (v. 3c); "But has not seen goodness" (v. 6a). Their hands, homes, and barns are filled with plenty, but their soul is empty. All they have accumulated has failed to bring them "goodness" (i.e., "soul satisfaction").

They are robbed of a decent burial, "Indeed, he has no burial" (v. 3d). Having no burial was a great curse and dishonor. This could mean that they have lost so much of their wealth through bad investments that they have no financial means for a decent burial at their death. This could also mean that the people they leave it to are so covetous that they will not spend the money to give them a decent burial.

A still-born child is better off than a covetous person (Vv. 3e – 5). "I say that a stillborn child is better than he" (v. 3e). This is a child that is taken from the womb to the grave. "Better is the fruit that drops from the tree before it is ripe than that which is left to hang on till it is rotten."[1]   When   Job   was experiencing adversity, he said a still-born child was better off than he (Job 3: 16). Solomon here says that a stillborn child is better off than they who have great prosperity and are covetous.

The sad condition of the stillborn: (Vv. 4, 5a). They come into the world "with vanity." The world considers he that is born, and dies immediately, as born in vain. "For it comes in vanity and departs in darkness" (v. 4a). Hardly any notice is taken of them. Their name is soon forgotten, "Its name is covered with darkness" (4b).They are born in darkness, never see light, and are buried in darkness, "Though it has not seen the sun or known anything" (v. 5a). They die ignorant. The sad condition of the stillborn is preferred over that of the covetous, "This has more rest than that man" (v. 5b). The person who lives in willful ignorance of God, and does not honor God with his life, is no better off than the stillborn. At least the stillborn has "rest," but not the selfish person.

He adds, "Do not all go to one place?" (v 6c).. The person who lives a 100 years goes to the same place as the child who lives for one hour. The grave is a place where we will all meet. No matter how conditions of men may differ in this life, all will die and go to the grave. The grave is to all, rich or poor, a place of silence, darkness, and separation from the living. "It is the common rendezvous of rich and poor, honorable and mean, learned and unlearned; the short-lived and long-lived meet in the grave, only one rides post thither, the other goes by a slower conveyance; the dust of both mingles, and lies undistinguished."[2]

Wealth itself will never bring happiness (Vv. 7 – 10). Four reasons are given. First, no matter how much one accumulates in this life, they will be unsatisfied (v. 7). There is nothing that "things" can do to satisfy a craving soul. It is impossible for material things to satisfy the spiritual hunger of man. This is why a little will serve to sustain us comfortably, and a great deal can do no more. Those that have an abundance of this world are still craving... "the soul is not satisfied." A person may feast today on "things" of today, but he will still be hungry for the "things of God" tomorrow.

Second, a poor man can live as well as a wise man (v. 8). Many wise men have known little more of real satisfaction than the poor. Many poor people have gained understanding, and have learned to face life. It is better to be poor and learn to live with one's circumstances, than to have much and be driven with such a strong desire for more that the joys of life are missed.

Third, the more a man has, the more is craved (v. 9). It is better to stop and enjoy what can be seen than to be always striving for what cannot be found (i.e., more of this world). Of course, it is much better to fix your eyes on the things of God.

Fourth, no matter how much a man gains, he is and will always be mere "man" (v. 10). The word "man" is the Hebrew word for "Adam." The thought is that no gains of this life will ever change the frailty of man. He will always be "man," no matter what his successes. It will do no good for frail man to "contend" with God over this. The word "contend" is the word used for fighting a case in a courtroom. Man is not sufficient for such a controversy with God.

The Foolishness of Trying
to Find Happiness in this World
(Vv. 11, 12)

Life itself is vanity, "Since there are many things that increase vanity" (v. 11a). Life itself will not satisfy the questions of a man's heart.

An abundance of possessions do not take a man closer to happiness, "How is man the better?" (v. 11b)

A man does not know what is best for him, because when he finally gains what he craved for, it fails to bring him satisfaction, "For who knows what is good for man in life" (v. 12a). It is like a child who cries for a knife, not realizing the harm it could bring. Likewise, man demands things from God, never considering whether it is in the purposes of God for him.

A man cannot take confidence in the continuance of life, "All the days of his vain life which he passes like a shadow?" (v. 12b) Life is so fleeting, transitory, and uncertain.

A man cannot consider anything in this world as certain, "Who can tell a man what will happen after him under the sun?" (v. 12c). A man cannot see the future, and will never know what happens in this world after his death.

CHAPTER SEVEN

"Separation and Sorrow"

Secrets for Separating
from the Vanity of this World
(Vv. 1 – 22)

Solomon is looking at the harder side of life. He is saying that the pleasant and the joyous are not always the best indication of life's truest meaning. It is very possible to learn more in the school of suffering than in the school of laughter. A person "may learn more in death than in life, in fasting than in feasting, in pain than in pleasure, in mourning than in mirth, in the rebuke of the wise than in the flattery of a fool, in patient endurance than in pride of spirit, in forbearance than in anger... feasting, fun, and flattery are much like the fire that comes from dried thorns. They are of little value for cooking or for sustenance of life against the cold. The thorns give their warmth quickly and intensely, but immediately their benefits are gone. The deeper and better lessons of life are often to be found in life's darker moments, in the experiences that most would shun if given opportunity. It is these moments that bring us back to reality and enable us to see things as they are (v. 10). Better to suffer lack and pain with understanding than to enjoy gifts that rob one of true perspective (v. 7)."[1]

He gives seven instructions:

First, maintain a good reputation (v. 1). A good (Hebrew – "better") name is worth more than all the world's wealth, "A good name is better than precious ointment" (v. 1a). The ointment (oil) speaks here of all the wealth of the world. Oil in those days was considered of great value. It speaks of the delights of our senses (ointment and perfume rejoice the heart, and is called "the oil of gladness"). It speaks of the honors and titles of man, and for which kings are anointed. A good name is worth more than all these. Proverbs 22:1, "A good name is rather to be chosen than great riches, and loving favor rather than silver and gold." A good name will bring us much more success and wealth in this life than all the world's wealth.

The day of death is better than the day of birth, "And the day of death than the day of one's birth" (v. 1b). Our going out of this world is a greater kindness to us than our coming into the world. Death puts an end to all the sorrows and grief of life. Death ushers us into eternal bliss (for those who have a good name). The day of our birth clogged our souls with the burden of the flesh. The day of our death will set us free from the flesh; the day of our death will set us free from this fleshly burden (Psalm 116: 15).

Secondly, be more serious minded (Vv. 2 – 6). According to these verses, "It is better to go to the house of mourning," and to "weep with those who weep" (Romans 12: 15), "than to go to the house of feasting," to a party, and "rejoice with those that do rejoice" (Romans 12: 15). It will be of greater benefit to us. Both are good. Jesus went to both a wedding at Cana and a funeral. Due to our tendency to be so earthly-minded, proud, and secure, it is better for us to share the sorrow and grief of a funeral. Dealing with death shows us the vanity of life.

Being serious minded has its benefits (Vv. 2, 4). It will supply us with information (v. 2a). We will see that death "is the end of all men." We will see that just as others have died, so will we. We will think about the fact of death and be challenged to serve God better, "And the living will lay it to heart" (v. 2b). Death can be a better sermon than that which is said behind pulpits. It will develop our character (v. 4). It will make us to be more serious about life. It will make us wiser (only a fool constantly lives in joy and laughter, never facing the seriousness of life). It will make us more compassionate for the suffering and sorrowful.

Being serious minded is better for us (v. 3). It is true that sorrow tends to turn our hearts more toward God, and laughter tends toward carnality.

Wise rebukes are better than foolish songs (Vv. 5, 6). We all love praise from the wise, but we shun their wise rebukes (v. 5). Proverbs 6:23, "Reproofs of instruction are the way of life." The rebukes of the wise may not be as pleasant as the song of fools, but they are much more wholesome. To listen to and receive the rebuke of the wise shows wisdom, but to delight in fools' songs shows a lack of sense. In Psalm 141: 5 David desired for his friends to reprove him for that which was wrong about him. He knew the honest reproofs of his friends would help bring him to repentance and healing, "It will be an excellent oil" to cure the wounds and bruises caused by sin (Proverbs 27: 6).

"The laughter of a fool" is compared to the burning "of thorns under a pot" (v. 6). They make a lot of noise and fire for a short while, but are quickly gone, turned to ashes, and produce no lasting heat that is required to cook food. "The laughter of fools" is noisy and flashy, but has no substance and deceives people because it lacks any real benefit or quality.

Third, be calm in spirit (Vv. 7 – 10). We are tempted not to be calm in spirit (Vv. 7, 8a). When we are constantly oppressed and troubled, we are tempted to grow embittered because of the constancy of it and complain against God, "Surely oppression destroys a wise man's reason" (v. 7a). Psalm 125:3 tells us that when even the wisest of saints endure hardships, it is difficult for them to control their spirits from foolish actions. Then there is the temptation to be "bribed," i.e., to trade godly endurance for a carnal way of escape. This only destroys what God desires to accomplish, "And a bribe debases the heart" (v. 7b). We cannot allow ourselves to get upset over injustice, "The end of a thing is better than its beginning" (v. 8a). By faith we must see the ultimate end of all injustice and expect it with patience (Romans 5:3 – 5, Hebrews 12:11). It seems that oppression and injustice will go on forever; not so. One day God will stop it.

The way to be calm in spirit (Vv. 8b – 10)... Be clothed with humility, "The proud in spirit" (v. 8b). The proud are those who cannot bear the trials and the misunderstandings of life. Pride is what keeps us from "bearing," thus we "break." Those who are humble toward God trust Him even though the trial is severe, and they do not understand (Mark 4: 16, 17). Be patient, "The patient in spirit" (v. 8c). Patiently trust God to work it out in His own time (James 1: 12). Govern your passions (v. 9). If we refuse to wait and be patient, and become upset at delays, then we will be angry when answers do not immediately come. If anger comes your way, let it pass away, for "anger rests in the bosom of fools." Only a fool will entertain anger in his heart, and grow embittered. A wise man gets and keeps it out of his heart. Make the best of the present (v. 10). We should not take for granted that the former days were any better than these. Nor should we inquire what is the reason for things, always demanding to know why. Note: "For you do not inquire wisely concerning this." When we must know the reason for all things, this shows an incompetent trust in God's sovereignty. To say that times past were better than these is foolish. How do we know? We were not there. Remember: times are evil, because man is evil. If man would mend, so would the times. We will not always know "the cause," but we can trust our all-wise God.

Fourth, be wise in all affairs (Vv. 11, 12, 19). He lists five reasons. 1. This is necessary for the proper management of possessions… "wisdom is good with an inheritance." An inheritance is of little good if you lack wisdom (v. 11a). Even though a person has an inheritance, if they do not have wisdom, it would have been better if they would have never had it. Wisdom is not only necessary for the poor so they may be content with what they have, but wisdom is necessary for the rich, also, so they can enjoy and use properly their riches. Wisdom teaches a person how to "make friends to himself" with their riches (Luke 16: 9). 2. This is necessary to gain advantage, "And profitable to those who see the sun" (v. 11b). Wisdom teaches a person how to use their possessions and talents to greatest advantage in this life. 3. Wisdom is necessary for safety and shelter, "For wisdom is a defense as money is a defense" (v. 12a). Wisdom enables a person to use their riches as a defense against trouble and the unexpected. The lack of wisdom will cause a person to "spend all," and have nothing for emergencies. 4. This is necessary because it brings true joy and happiness, "But the excellence of knowledge is that wisdom gives life to those who have it" (v. 12b). Wealth can bring heartache. Wisdom brings happiness. 5. This is necessary because it strengthens and supports (v. 19).

Wisdom makes a person strong in spirit, bold, and resolute. Wisdom gains a person friends and a good reputation. Wisdom gives a person strength in suffering and sorrow. Wisdom makes one man stronger than ten unwise men.

Fifth, be submitted to the will of God (Vv. 13 - 15). See the hand of God in all things (v. 13), "Consider the work of God" (v. 13a). This will stop us from complaining about things we do not understand, and prevent us from speaking against things that are God's doings. We must see all things, good and bad, as "the work of God," and consider "all things" as His eternal purpose to be fulfilled in our life. We must "by faith" believe that every work of God is wise, just, and good. There is harmony and beauty in all His works, and will eventually appear to have been for the best. We must then give thanks in all things, and endeavor to allow Him to serve His purposes. "For who can make straight what He has made crooked?" (v. 13b) We cannot change anything that God has determined. If He allows trouble, it is not in our power to make peace. If He allows a bewildering incident, which of us can understand it? Since we cannot change God's purposes, we should trust them.

Submit to the various ways God leads (v. 14). When prosperity comes our way, we should enjoy it. But when adversity comes, we must "consider" it (v. 14a). "Consider" speaks of "thoughtfulness, reflection." "Surely God has appointed the one as well as the other" (v, 14b). There is a fine line between adversity and prosperity, and we can easily pass from one to another. The reason for all this is given, "So that man can find out nothing that will come after him" (v. 14c). This means that we will not fix our heart on this constantly changing world, but on our never-changing God. The truth here is that prosperity and adversity come from the hand of God. They are so narrowly separated that we can easily pass from one to the other. When prosperity comes, we should have self-controlled joy. When adversity comes, we should "consider" it, i.e., learn something from it! The purpose of prosperity and adversity is to show us how transient they are, and cause us to fix our hearts on God in all things with submission and trust.

Don't get upset over the prosperity of the wicked, or the suffering of the saints (v. 15). It will always be an enigma as to why the righteous perish and the wicked live on in their prosperity. However, one thing we do know is that the calamities of the righteous are preparing them for an eternity with God, while the wicked are ripening for ruin. The truth is, we will never fully understand why the righteous perish and the wicked prosper. However, we can avoid hasty conclusions and immature, unconsidered, and partial judgments. We will always be confronted with things we cannot comprehend. Our observation is so limited! Our reasoning is faulty! This does not mean that we are to shut our eyes to the facts of life and act as fatalists, but we are to think, trust, and wait.

Sixth, avoid all dangerous extremes (Vv. 16 – 18). We do this three ways. 1. We must persevere in acts of righteousness, but at the same time refrain from extremism (v. 16). Sometimes, in our zeal toward righteousness, we become extreme in it, thus causing ourselves trouble. All our acts of righteousness should be governed by wisdom and prudence. "In how many instances may it be observed that a person is no sooner convinced that a certain object is desirable, a certain course is to be approved, than he will hear and think of nothing else? Is liberty good? Then away with all restraints! Is self-denial good? Then away with all pleasures! Is the Bible the best of books? Then let no other volume be opened! Calm reason would check such a tendency, but the voice of reason is silenced by passion or prejudice. Impulsive natures are hurried into unreasoning, extravagant opinions and habits of conduct. The momentum of a powerful emotion is very great; it may urge men onwards to an extent unexpected and dangerous. While under the guidance of sober reason, feeling may be the motive power to virtue and usefulness, but when uncontrolled it may hurry into folly and disaster."[2]

2. Sinners must refrain from extreme sin if they do not choose to live for God (v. 17). Though some men are wicked, there is still some sin they will not indulge in because of the fear of God, hell, etc. The words "do not be overly wicked" mean "do not be foolish and aggravate your sinfulness, lest God destroy you before your time." "This does not advocate that anyone can be a little wicked, but that one must not add

more sin to his life of ungodliness which is already condemned, for doing so could bring judgment before it would come otherwise – in due time."[3]

3. Wisdom will keep us balanced, avoiding extremes (v. 18). "It is good that you grasp this" means "get wisdom and retain it!" "And also not remove your hand from the other, for he who fears God will escape them all" means "the person who walks in wise trust in God, avoiding extremes will have a much better understanding and balanced view of life."

Seventh, we are to be mild and tender toward those who have hurt us (Vv. 19 – 22). Three ways to do this:

1. We are not to expect perfection from people (Vv. 19, 20). The ones who keep this in mind are not aggravated by people's faults and imperfections. They

Realize they are dealing with frail human beings (v. 19). Even the best of men have their faults (sins) (v. 20). I Kings 8:46, "For there is no one who does not sin. "Proverbs 20:9, "Who can say, I have made my heart clean, I am pure from my sin?"

2. We are to overlook the way people mistreat us (v. 21). We are not to get so upset over things said about us (Psalm 38: 12 – 15). We are not to be inquisitive to know what people say about us. If they say good things it will feed our pride, and if they say bad things it will make us angry. This is good to remember, for there is probably a great deal more evil said of us than we think there is by people whom we least suspect.

3. We are to remember our own faults (v. 22). We become upset over the very things we

have been guilty of doing (Titus 3: 2, 3; James 3: 1, 2; Matthew 7: 1, 2).

Solomon's Sorrow for His Sin
(Vv. 23 – 29)

In the previous verses Solomon proved the vanity of this world and its inability to make men happy. Now he shows the vileness of sin and how it makes men miserable.

He sorrows over his limited wisdom (Vv. 23 – 25a). He says he searched diligently for wisdom (Vv. 23, 25a). He was determined to be wise, "All this I have proved by wisdom" (v. 23a). He was diligent in his pursuit for wisdom, "I applied my heart to know, to search and seek out wisdom and the reason of all things" (v. 25a). His diligent and determined search for wisdom is commendable! Sadly, his search for wisdom did not satisfy (Vv. 23b, 24). He attempted to be fully wise, to know all things, but the vastness of wisdom was too much for him, "But it was far from me" (v. 23b). The more he knew, the more he discovered was to be known. He was not able to fully understand God, His ways and counsels … "that which is far off, and exceedingly deep, who can find it out?" (v. 24) God was too great for him, a mere man, to understand (Psalm 145: 3; Romans 11: 33).

He sorrows over his unlimited sin (Vv. 25b – 29). He speaks of the depths of his sin, "To know the wickedness of folly, even of foolishness and madness" (v. 25b). Solomon took great pains to know the depths of sin. He says his sin was "folly," saying that his "folly" was "wicked." He says it was "foolishness" and "madness" to ever engage in sin like he did. Willful sinners are foolish and mad. They act contrary to right reason and to their true interest.

He speaks of the result of his experience with sin (Vv. 26 – 29). Solomon discovered the sinfulness of that great sin which he had been guilty, "But King Solomon loved many strange women" (1 Kings 11: 1). How evil it is, "And I find more bitter than death" (v. 26a). He discovered the grief of remembering his sin, because it grieved him, burdened his conscience, and agonized him when he thought upon the wickedness and foolishness of his actions. His sin terrorized him when He thought upon it, bringing shame to his memory. Proverbs 5: 9, 11 speaks of the horrors of immorality.

He discovered the dangerous temptation to sin... "the woman whose heart is snares and nets" (v. 26b). He says that it is nearly impossible for those that venture into temptation to escape the sin, and for those that have fallen into the sin to be delivered except through repentance. Sin lays "snares and nets," says Solomon to catch its victims. People are enticed into sin with the bait of pleasure. They "take the bait," and are sometimes temporarily satisfied with it. Then they soon realize they are trapped in it, as in a net... "and her hands are fetters." Sin's fond embrace are actually chains of bondage (Proverbs 5: 22).

He discovered that we are only kept from sin by the grace of God, "He who pleases God will escape from her" (v. 26c). Those that are not bound by sin must realize it is not by any strength of their own, but by the grace of God. Those that would be free must realize it is an impossible situation within themselves, but not with God... if they will please Him (i.e., keep His word). The word "escape" means "be smooth like cement or mortar; give council or deliver (as one's deliverance); be saved by the skin of your teeth" (Job 19: 20).

He discovered that the person who continues in sin will get worse, "But the sinner shall be trapped by her" (v. 26d). They will be led step by step into deeper sin as their minds slowly become debauched and their conscience seared. The person who goes this way will be turned over to his depths of sin (Romans 1: 26, 28; Ephesians 4: 18, 19).

He discovered how corrupt man's nature is (Vv. 27 – 29). He sought to discover how much he had sinned (v. 27). He actually wanted to number his sins one by one, so he might one by one receive forgiveness and cleansing. The more particular the repentance, the more peaceful the pardon. Also, the discovery of one sin leads to the discovery of more (Job 34:32).

He discovered this was impossible, for his sins were innumerable (v. 28). "Which my soul seeks, but cannot find" means he found that the more he counted, the more there was to count (Jeremiah 17: 9, 10; Psalm 19: 12). He says he was only able to find "one man among a thousand" that was good. Everyone has corruption, for, "But a woman among all these I have not found." There was not one woman in a thousand who was what a woman ought to be. Solomon had a thousand wives and concubines and his experience might well have been that mentioned in these words.

He concludes that man sins because he was born in corruption (v. 29). God made man "upright." Man corrupted himself…man sins because he is corrupt. God made man sinless, but he "sought out many scheme" – "devices, or ways of sinning."

CHAPTER EIGHT

"Wisdom"

In this chapter, Solomon recommends wisdom as the most powerful antidote against the vanity of this world.

The Benefits of Wisdom
(V. 1)

True wisdom is invaluable. To gain wisdom is to be a good man. Wisdom enables a man to know God, thus he knows and understands himself (Proverbs 4:7).

Wisdom exalts a person, "Who is like a wise man?" (v. 1a) A wise man advances above others, because he is more excellent than his peers. A wise man knows that, along with his "charisma," he must have "character" if he is to succeed.

Wisdom makes a person important, "And who knows the interpretation of a thing?" (v. 1b) The word "interpretation" means "solution." A wise man is an important man, because he has solutions. He understands the times and events of things, thus he is able to give direction. 1 Chronicles 12: 32, "And the children of Issachar, which were men that had understanding of the times to know what Israel ought to do" (Matthew 16: 1 – 4; Matthew 24: 36 – 39).

Wisdom brings a man honor, "A man's wisdom makes his face shine" (v. 1c). In Exodus 34:29, we read where Moses' face shone. The word "shine" means "will enlighten, illuminate." "The serene light within makes itself visible in the outward expression; the man is contented and cheerful and shows this in his look and bearing"[1] Wisdom beautifies a man in the eyes of his friends. It adds radiance to his conversation. It causes him to be taken notice of and respected. "It scarcely needs a proof that the countenance or front of the head is regarded in Scripture as the mirror or divine influences upon the man – of all affections, and of the entire life of soul and spirit. In the physiognomy (facial features) is reflected the moral condition of the man."[2]

Romans 5: 3 - 5 gives additional insight to "the shining face." Paul wrote, "We glory in tribulations, knowing that tribulation produces perseverance, and perseverance, character, and character, hope. Now hope does not disappoint, because the love of God has been poured out in our hearts by the Holy Spirit who was given to us." The word "tribulations" means "pressures, or crushings." This word came from the use of the olive and wine press in the Old Testament. When the olive or grape went into the press, it was crushed because there was a desired quality in it, oil or wine. Until the olive or grape was crushed, the juice or oil could not be released. By passing through the press, the desired quality was released and became usable and enjoyable to others. We are to "glory in tribulations." We are never usable to the Lord until we are emptied of pride and self. There is no short cut to spiritual reality. There must be a pressing and a crushing.

Oil and wine are symbolic of the presence of God in the Old Testament. Not until we have passed through "tribulation" is that desired quality released from our life. Psalm 104: 15 is a reference to both "oil" and "wine." Wine makes our heart glad, symbolic of the Holy Spirit, who fills us with heaven's joy, as we are more emptied of self (Ephesians 5: 18-20). Oil makes the face to shine. Oil was both a medicine and a cosmetic in Bible times. It was primarily a cosmetic to make the face to shine. A shining face meant a person was more attractive. Numbers 6: 24, 25 states that God has a shining face. Moses prayed that Aaron would receive a shining face from the Lord. He knew that anyone who beheld the Lord of the shining face would come away with a shining face.

II Corinthians 3: 18, "But we all, with unveiled face, beholding as in a mirror the glory of the Lord, are being transformed into the same image from glory to glory, just as by the Spirit of the Lord." We are to behold the glory of the Lord with an unveiled face. As God's shining face begins to radiate upon us, we are changed into the same image. The God of a shining face desires to produce a people of a shining face. He places us in "tribulation" to produce "wisdom," as he removes our veils of pride, ego, self, etc., through pressures and crushings.

This is why Paul said in Romans 5: 3, "We also glory in tribulations." Tribulations (crushings, pressures) release that desired quality within us (oil - glory of the Lord; wine - fullness of the Holy Spirit) by breaking the outer shell of make believe (self, ego, masks that we hide behind).. From this wisdom comes – "patience, experience," "hope," and "love." This wisdom "makes our face to shine" (Ecclesiastes 8: 1).

"Many a poet, and seer, and martyr, and reformer, and woman of the finest fiber has, at times, had a face that has looked like porcelain with a light behind it"[3]

Wisdom gives a man boldness, "And the sternness of his face is changed" (v. 1d).

Wisdom will strengthen and uphold a man when he is being attacked by his adversaries. Wisdom will prevent a man from becoming "shaken" and "panicky" in times of turmoil. Proverbs 1: 24 – 33 is an admonition and a warning from wisdom (Proverbs 16: 16).

Some Words of Wisdom
(Vv. 2 – 17)

Obey the government God has set over us (Vv. 2 – 5). Five instructions are given. First, we are to obey the laws (v. 2). The words "I say" could mean "I charge you." Unless a law of the land violates the commandments of God, we are to obey the laws, even if it means suffering and hardship (Romans 13: 1 – 7; Titus 3: 1; 1 Peter 2: 13 – 15). Exceptions to obedience to the law of the land is found with Moses' parents

(Hebrews 11 : 23), Daniel and his friends (1:8; 3 : 16 - 18; 6 : 10), and the apostles before the Sanhedrin (Acts 4: 19, 20). In each of these cases, to obey the law would have meant to disobey God. Where no divine ordinance is violated by obeying the civil law, the Christian is to obey. Remember – the bad citizen cannot be a good Christian.

Second, we are not to sit in judgment on the government authority, "Do not be hasty to go from his presence" (v. 3a). We are not to quarrel with everything that is not done exactly to our liking. We are not to cast off our allegiance to those over us when something is done contrary to our thinking. God expects us to be loyal and retain our commitment (allegiance), even if everything does not please us. This is true in all walks of life, such as the local church, marriage, government, employment, etc.

Third, we are not to be involved in acts of rebellion, "Do not take your stand for an evil thing, for he does whatever pleases him" (v. 3b). We are not to join with those who rebel against God's authority. The words "do not take your stand" mean "persist not in an evil affair" ("conspiracy, insurrection"). The reason is given "for he does whatever pleases him." The thought is of an irresponsible monarch who does what he wants, regardless of the people's wishes and wants, regardless of the people's wishes and actions.

Fourth, reasons for obeying the delegated authority (Vv. 4, 5a)... Those in positions of authority have the power, "Where the word of a king is there is power" (v. 4a). Those in positions of authority have absolute power, "And who may say to him, 'what are you doing?'" (v. 4b) Obedience brings peace, "He who keeps his command will experience nothing harmful" (v. 5a). The word "experience" means "will know," i.e., experience no disturbance (Hebrews 13:7, 17.)

Fifth, we are to choose the wisest opportunity to disagree when disagreement is necessary, "And a wise man's heart discerns both time and judgment" (v. 5b). The words "time and judgment" mean "the time and the way." There is a proper time and way to express disagreement.

Be prepared for unexpected evils and death by trusting God (Vv. 6 – 8). In verse 5, the Scriptures tells how a person can be successful by developing an ability to "discern time and judgment." However, the truth is, very few people have that ability to foresee an event. Thus, all are "caught off guard" at times, and this is why we must prepare for the unexpected.

Four reasons:

First, because all events are determined by the foreknowledge of God... "Because for every matter there is a time and judgment" (v. 6a). Knowing this, we may be at peace and rest, trusting our heavenly Father, because He does all things well, and cannot make a mistake. Our responsibility is to be faithful in our callings, not to become "weary in well doing" (Galatians 6: 9), and to trust "events" to our God.

Second, because we cannot avoid the unexpected, for we have no way of knowing what is coming... "Though the misery of man increases greatly" (v. 6b). We do not know what events may befall us "tomorrow," and, because of this, it is difficult to know what decisions to make today. In these words, "because to every matter there is" only one way, one method, one proper opportunity, "though the misery of man increases greatly," Scripture is saying that it is extremely difficult to know what tomorrow will bring. Because of this difficulty, it is nearly impossible to plan for it! This is one thing that contributes to a person's misery.

Third, we do not have the ability to know the future (v. 7). There is no way for feeble man to foresee the future. We do not know what tomorrow holds (Matthew 6 34; James 4 13-16).

Fourth, because no matter what other evils we may avoid, we cannot avoid dying (v. 8). There is nothing we can do about dying, "No one has power over the spirit to retain the spirit, and no one has power in the day of death" (v. 8a). Actually, this is saying, "We have no power over the day of our death." When our soul is required of God, it will resign. No arguments, disputes, objections, etc., will delay it. When our appointed time comes, we will die. We will all die sooner or later, "There is no release from that war" (v. 8b). One day we will all face our war (battle) with death. This is a confrontation we will all have – there is no avoidance of it. No one can resist death, "And wickedness will not deliver those who are given to it" (v. 8c). Men use wickedness to help them avoid the realities of life and death. They will engage in almost anything that will help them momentarily escape thoughts of dying and facing God. They fail to realize that the very things they trust to deliver them from death will deliver them up to death.

Don't be disturbed by oppressive authority (Vv. 9 – 13). Oppressive rulers only cause hurt (v. 9). They hurt those over whom they rule. According to Romans 13: 4, those in authority are, 'the ministers of God to you for good" (not hurt and harm). This must be remembered by anyone in authority over others, they "rule" for "the good" of their subjects. However, oppressive rulers do just the opposite, they hurt (Ephesians 6: 9; 1 Timothy 4: 12; 1 Peter 5: 1 – 4). They also hurt themselves. Oppressive rulers are not respected, or appreciated.   Eventually, their oppression of others will backlash on them. Those in authority must remember this.

Oppressive rulers prosper as they abuse their power (v. 10). They go into power having very little, but soon have great wealth. They continue in this extravagance all the days of their reign. The day comes when these rulers who lived in wealth, die in wealth, and have an expensive funeral. But note what soon happens, "And they were forgotten in the city where they had so done." The very people with whom they were so popular soon forgot them!

Oppressive rulers become more wicked in their prosperity (v. 11). Just because God's judgment on sin does not immediately come, people think it will never come. This seeming delay in God's judgment causes them to become more evil in their sin. People become disillusioned into thinking that "God is not as harsh toward evil as has always been claimed" and they scoff at the thought of accountability, judgment day and the lake of fire. Note the word "heart." This is the seat of thought and the prime mover of action. This "heart" becomes "fully set in them to do evil." Their heart becomes filled with every kind of thought that is evil. As they do not experience God's wrath, judgment, etc., they become more brash and embolden with their sin. However, they forget that to trample on God's mercy is a greater wickedness than to break

His law (Isaiah 5: 18 – 25). Ezekiel 18: 4 says judgment has already been pronounced. It is delayed only by grace. "Though the mills of God grind slowly, yet they grind exceeding small; though with patience He stands waiting, He exactly judgeth all." Judgment deferred is not judgment abandoned!

Oppressive rulers will be punished (Vv. 12, 13). Even though oppressed, those who please God will be happy (v. 12). Even if it does not presently seem like it, God's people (those who please Him) will eventually "come out on top." Even though severely troubled with hardships, a person who will faithfully please God will have an inner peace, for he knows that all is right with God. This is something we can have confidence in ("I surely know"). Even though very prosperous, those who disobey God are miserable (v. 13). Their days (life) are so uncertain, "as a shadow," empty and meaningless. They will miss everlasting life, "...nor will he prolong his days." They have made themselves to be an enemy of a loving God, "he does not fear before God."

Don't be disturbed over the prosperity of the wicked and troubles of the righteous (Vv. 14 – 17). It has always been an enigma how the prosperity of the wicked and the troubles of the righteous can be reconciled with the holiness and goodness of God as He governs the world. These Scriptures advise us on this matter. We should not be surprised by it as though it were something new (v. 14a, b). Just men have always suffered, "There is a vanity which occurs on earth, that there are just men to whom it happens according to the work of the wicked" (v. 14a). The word "happens" means "to come to," to "strike against." This means that sometimes the "just" suffer the evils that the wicked deserve. The truth is that good men often suffer the consequences of other people's evil deeds, and bad men reap the benefits of other people's good works (Hebrews 11: 35 – 40).

Unjust men have always prospered, "Again, there are wicked men to whom it happens according to the work of the righteous" (v. 14b). Wicked men have prospered as though they pleased God. Their prosperity seems to be contradictory to the warnings of Scripture. We see the godly troubled and perplexed in their minds, and the wicked happy and secure. This is hard to understand, but "faith" knows that while a man lives and carries out his purposes, God is carrying out His purposes through them (Job 34: 10, 11). God's thoughts are deep, His works are vast and His way past finding out (Psalm 77: 19; Romans 11: 33).

We should not fault God with it, "I said that this also is vanity" (v. 14c). We should not accuse God of doing wrong, but recognize the "vanity which occurs on earth." This enigma of "why do the righteous suffer and the wicked prosper" is not the fault of God, but the cruelty of this earth. God may reign supreme, but He honors man's "will," thus the unfairness in this world is caused by the "will of man." Man attempts to blame God, but man is the one who is guilty! There is "vanity which occurs on earth," but God offers an eternal home of eternal bliss. The vanity (unfairness) of this earth should set our hearts on Heaven.

We must learn to be content with God's will for our life (v. 15). The words "so I commanded enjoyment" ("joy") mean "a holy security and serenity of mind, arising from a confidence in God, His power, His providence, and His promises ." The words "because a man has nothing better under the sun than to eat, drink, and be merry" mean "we should thankfully enjoy the good things God has given us, and don't upset ourselves over injustices of life and things about God's providence we do not understand." "For this will remain with him in his labor all the days of his life which God gives him under the sun" mean "the happiest thing for us to do is to make the best of what we have, and be cheerful and content with our position in life."

We must understand that this is an enigma that no one will ever understand (Vv. 16, 17). Many have tried to understand (v. 16). They diligently seek to understand, as did Solomon, "When I applied my heart to know wisdom and to see the business that is done on earth" (v. 16a). They worry and lose sleep over it, as did Solomon, "Even though one sees no sleep day or night" (v. 16b). This speaks of the sleeplessness of the one who meditates on and tries to solve all the problems, injustices, and disorders of life. It has all been futile attempts (v. 17). We can look upon the work of God, and try to establish a pattern God follows so we may understand all He does... but it will be futile. Men have "labored" to find an answer, and "wise men" have studied it, all in futility. In Isaiah 55: 6 – 13, we are given the reason why.

CHAPTER NINE

"Four Observations"

Solomon gives us four observations in this chapter to further show us the vanity of this world.

First, good men and bad men experience basically the same things in life (Vv. 1 – 3).

The thing that Solomon observed in life was the way both "the good" and "the bad" experience the same sorrows and joys. This has been a stumbling block for generations. It has been said, "Life is a comedy to those who think, a tragedy to those who feel." What this means is that men have grown discouraged and sorrowful over unanswered events of life when they see oppression come to "the good," just as it does to "the bad." They "feel" (i.e., try to figure it all out), instead of "think" (i.e., trust God in life's enigmas). In this chapter, Solomon does not give us all the answers, but he does give us enough information to accept contentedly what we cannot understand. He says, "For I considered all this in my heart (v. 1a). Before he spoke, he deliberated in his heart. There is a good lesson here. What we are to declare, we should first consider. We should think twice before we speak once (Proverbs 15:23).

God has a special care and concern for His people, "That the righteous and the wise and their works are in the hand of God" (v. 1b). This means they are in God's power and under His direction (Psalm 31: 15; Proverbs 21:1). They are under His protection and guidance. All their affairs are managed by Him for their good. All their righteous actions "are in the hand of God" to be rewarded in the "other world," though not in this. It may seem that they are in the hands of the enemy at times, but not so. The events that affect them do not come to pass by chance, but all according to the will and counsel of God, which will turn what seemed to be against them to be for them. Whatever happens, all of God's people are in His hand (Deuteronomy 33:3; John 10: 29). This is the way God's people adjust to difficulty. In Job 24:1, Job spoke of God's omniscience. Jeremiah spoke of God's righteousness (Jeremiah 12:1-3). Also, in Psalm 73:1, the Psalmist spoke of God's faithful goodness to His people. This is what Solomon wants to present. Good and evil comes to all men, but God has a special care for His own true people.

God's dealings cannot be judged by man's outward condition, "People know neither love nor hatred by anything they see before them" (v. 1c). No one can judge from the events that befall a person what view God has of his character. It is as unfair as were Job's friends to decide that a man is a great sinner because trouble comes his way. It is a mistake to believe that because a person prospers that he is righteous. Outward circumstances are very weak evidences of a person's inward condition or eternal reward.

When we witness troubles or blessings in others, we have no right to argue God's displeasure or pleasure with them. God disposes events of life that best serve His eternal purposes. We must not expect everyone to be treated as we have judged they should be. In Proverbs 1: 32, Scripture speaks of a fool prospering. Hebrews 12: 6 speaks of a child of God being chastened.

All things come alike to all (v. 2). There is no difference in life's treatment of "all." Good and evil comes to "all." "All" have the sun, shade, rain, storm, etc. The righteous do not necessarily experience greater prosperity than the wicked. The person who serves God many times experiences the same calamity as the one who despises God. There is no thunderbolt of vengeance consistently smiting the wicked. Sometimes the righteous are cut off in their prime while the wicked enjoy a long life. Though "all things come alike to all," there is a distinction between the righteous and the wicked. The righteous are "clean," and the wicked are "unclean." The righteous are morally undefiled. The wicked are immorally defiled. Though there may be no great difference in their condition here, there will be in the after-life. The righteous "sacrifice," the wicked "does not sacrifice." The righteous consciously worship and serve God. The wicked willfully despise God. The righteous are "good"... the wicked are "sinners." The righteous do good in this world and please God. The wicked violate God's law and displease Him. The righteous "fears an oath," but the wicked "takes an oath." The righteous reverences God, His word, His name. The wicked show no true reverence for God, His word, His name. The person who is "righteous" is different, even in this world. Because of their righteousness, they place themselves under God's protection and blessing, a protection and a blessing the wicked know nothing of. There is little difference between the conditions of the righteous and the wicked, for "one event happens to the righteous and the wicked." Both prosper and are blessed.

Both face trouble and calamity. There is a difference between the design, nature, and purpose, though, of the same event to the one and to the other. The effects are also different. The one is to life; the other is to death.

This often causes the wise and good to be perplexed, "This is an evil in all that is done under the sun, that one thing happens to all" (v. 3a). Nothing has caused more disturbance than "one thing happens to all." No matter how much the wicked prosper, they will suffer. "Truly the hearts of the sons of men are full of evil; madness is in their hearts while they live, and after that they go to the dead" (v. 3b). No matter how much they prosper now, they are actually "madmen" ("madness is in their hearts while they live"). They conduct themselves in ways totally opposed to wisdom and reason. All of their lives, they follow their own lust and passion, with little regard for God's will and purposes. It is called "madness" (i.e., "want of reason"). They will soon die, "and after that they go to the dead." Though on this side the righteous and the wicked seem to be alike, they will not be on the other side!

Second, we should enjoy life before death ends it all (Vv. 4 – 10). Earlier, Solomon "praised the dead more than the living" (v. 4: 2). Here he considers the advantages of the living over the dead, and how the living can take advantage of life to prepare for death.

The living have advantages over the dead (Vv. 4 – 6). We still have "hope" (the dead do not), for while there is life "there is hope" (v. 4). The living still have the privilege of knowing, loving, and dealing with others. Though a person's condition is bad, yet, because he has life, "there is hope." Though a person is evil, yet, because he has life, "there is hope." Though a person has been cast aside as useless, "there is hope," for he still has life (a dead person has none of these advantages). Then he says, "For a living dog is better than a dead lion." In those days, in Palestine, the dog was not made a pet and companion, as they are today. They were regarded as a loathsome and despicable object (1 Samuel 17: 43; 2 Samuel 3: 8). The lion was considered to be a very noble beast, a symbol of greatness and power (Proverbs 30: 30; Isaiah 31: 4). So, what is meant here is the most rejected and despised person in life has greater hope and possibility than the most talented and gifted person who is dead.

We, the living, have an opportunity to prepare for death, while the dead do not, "For the living know that they will die" (v. 5a). The living, at least, have the consciousness that they will soon have to die. This causes them to work while it is day, and make use of every opportunity.

We can enjoy this life, but the dead cannot (Vv. 5b, c, d, 6). The dead lose all contact with this life, "But the dead know nothing" (v. 5b). They are cut off from this active, bustling world. They have no expectations, and nothing to work for. What happens on the earth does not affect them, and they have no knowledge of it (Job 10: 21, 22). The dead cannot enjoy this life, "And they have no more reward" (v. 5c). The dead are not remembered, "For the memory of them is forgotten" (v. 5d). To the people of that day, one of the tragedies of death was that it "wiped out" the memory of one's name. To those people to have their name remembered was a blessing much desired. Further, the dead do not enjoy their friends and companions anymore (v.6).

It is wise for the living to make the best use of life (Vv. 7 – 10). We should enjoy the comforts of life that come our way (Vv. 7 – 9). A person should make the best use of life while it lasts, and manage wisely what remains of it. The living are admonished to do so, "Go, eat your bread with joy, and drink your wine with a merry heart" (7a). The words "go" and "merry heart" are an admonishment to enjoy ourselves. We should enjoy our God, friends, and comforts. We should serve God with gladness, and use what He has given us. We are to make use of the comforts and enjoyments God has given us, and learn to be content with what we are given, and enjoy it - "eat your bread, drink your wine."

We are told to be bright and cheerful (v. 8). White garments are a symbol of joy and purity, speaking of positive, joyful people. Our relations are to be enjoyed, "Live joyfully with the wife whom you love all the days of your vain life which He has given you under the sun" (v. 9a). Live joyfully with your wife or husband that God has given you. "All the days of your vain life" mean "throughout the time of your quickly passing life." The living are reminded that to truly enjoy life, we must be right with God, "For God has already accepted your works" (v. 7b). This means that our life ("works") must be acceptable to God. The person who lives their life according to God's good pleasure is enjoying abundant life. There are reasons why we should enjoy life (v. 9b), because the living are going to have their share of griefs and troubles... "all your days are vanity." Life will bring trouble and disappointment. We will have enough of our time taken up by grief and sorrow. Our enjoyment of life will be a powerful antidote against life's heartaches. This life is only going to allow us a few joys and comforts anyway, "for that is your portion in life, and in the labor which you perform under the sun." In Heaven, the joys and comforts will be everlasting. Here, there are only a few passing years for joys and comforts.

We should become involved in the business of this life (v. 10). The living are to do good in this life, "Whatever your hand finds to do, do it with your might" (v. 10a). We are not to resign ourselves to fate, but to work to improve this world. All of our energies are to be used to carry out the purposes for our life. We should find the good that we can do ("your hand finds to do"), looking for life's opportunities. We should be willing to "pay the price" to reach our goals, and attain our opportunities (Proverbs 17: 16). We are to do good and do it diligently ("do it with your might"), taking advantage of our opportunities with vigor, care, and with determination, no matter what the difficulties. Remember, harvest days are busy days. What must be done must be done with much diligence. Finally, we are to do good while we have the opportunity, "For there is no work or device or knowledge or wisdom in the grave where you are going" (v. 10b). If the work God has given us is not done in our lifetime, it may never get done. Every day brings us one step closer to the grave. When we are in the grave, it will be too late – too late to get saved, too late to work for God, too late to fulfill God's calling (John 9:4).

Third, the future is so uncertain (Vv. 11, 12). To further demonstrate the vanity of this world, Solomon reminds us of the uncertainty of the future. He tells us how we make our plans, then our plans are interrupted by unforeseen events.

In verse 10, we are told that whatever we do, we must do "with all our might," but because we cannot control the future, we must leave the results to God.

Our dreams and hopes for the future are often disappointed (v. 11). Solomon had learned, as have so many others, that events do not always agree with our plans (i.e., things do not always work out as planned.) Because of these disappointments, we are driven to further dependence on God. We are given examples of how life's dreams and hopes are disappointed, "I returned and saw under the sun that the race is not to the swift, nor the battle to the strong, nor bread to the wise, nor riches to men of understanding, nor favor to men of skill" (v. 11a). The race is not always to the swift. One would think that the one who has the swiftest foot would always win the prize, but not so. An accident could prevent them from winning. Negligence could prevent them from attaining the prize. Just as swiftness of foot is no guarantee that a runner will be the first to reach the goal, so in other areas of life the possession of superior ability is no proof that a person will excel.

The greater army does not always win the battle. Logic would say that the larger, stronger army will prevail. History has proven that a smaller army that is well–trained and wisely prepared has often prevailed. A "weak" person, who will work hard, diligently apply themselves and be wise, can win life's battles. The wise do not always succeed. There are exceptions to the rule that says diligence is always rewarded. There are examples of people who should have excelled but they did not. The skillful are not always promoted. Many times a person of great skill and ability to make a lot of money do not have the ability to manage it. They know how to make money but they do not know how to manage money. Riches are no sign of wisdom. "Men of skill" have often been shunned and scorned by their generation, peers, company, etc., and fools received the recognition and promotion.

The disappointments are not because of "chance," but because of the providence of God, "But time and chance happen to them all" (v. 11b). The word "chance" in our English conveys a wrong impression. It means "incident," such as a calamity, disappointment, un-foreseen occurrence. All of a person's dreams and hopes are liable to be changed or controlled by events beyond their power, and which have no explanation. God is the One who is watching over life on this planet, and all of man's successes are totally dependent upon His higher laws which often bring unexpected results (Psalm 31: 15a).

Things happen that we are not prepared to handle (v. 12). We do not know what troubles await us, "For man also does not know his time" (v. 12a). With one sudden event, our aims can be frustrated, our anticipations clouded, and our efforts defeated. In a moment of time, we could meet with death, for none has the promise of tomorrow. We can have trouble with the very things we expected to enjoy, "Like fish taken in a cruel net, like birds caught in a snare, so the sons of men are snared in an evil time, when it falls suddenly upon them" (v. 12b). The suddenness and unforeseen nature of calamities that happen to people are here expressed by these two similes. The very thing that should have brought satisfaction to the fish and the birds proved to be a snare to them... they were suddenly caught in the net. Likewise, trouble is often found where a person thought they would find satisfaction. The "young man void of understanding" in Proverbs 7: 7, who thought he could find satisfaction with "the immoral woman" (Proverbs 7: 5), never realized that he was as a bird that hastens to the snare. Just as "he did not know it would cost his life" (Proverbs 7: 23), so often things we think will bring us pleasure can bring us heartache. The answer is Proverbs 3: 5, 6.

Fourth, wisdom makes a person useful, though often they will have little respect (Vv. 13 - 18). In verse 13, Solomon still recommends wisdom for a successful life. Even though he said, in verse 11... "nor bread to the wise," yet he still recognizes how valuable wisdom is.

He gives an example of this (Vv. 14, 15). He speaks of a man, though poor, who served his city in time of great danger and distress. "Now here was found in it a poor wise man, and he by his wisdom delivered the city" (v. 15a). A mighty king with a great and strong army came against "a little city" (v. 14a). The inhabitants were few... feeble, scared, and weak (v. 14b.) This king and his army surrounded the city, "and built great snares around it" (v. 14c). These "snares" were embankments, or mounds, raised high enough to go over the top of the city walls. They also served as a place to direct the besieging of the city. A citizen, though poor, arises to lead the weak and helpless defenders (v. 15a). He encouraged and inspired them. He gave them wise counsel as to how to be delivered. His wisdom, faith, fortitude and inspiration delivered them. Evidently, they had left him out of their planning sessions. Instead of bitterness and resentment, he overcame such immature reactions, and responded to the need by offering his wise assistance. Note: People who have been shunned and overlooked by their peers and superiors must not grow bitter, but remain wise and sweet in spirit, willing to help those who have mistreated them (Matthew 5:44). He reveals that because the man was poor they ignored him, "Yet no one remembered that same poor man" (v. 15b). As soon as the emergency had passed, the man went back to being insignificant. He received no honor, or token of appreciation. The very people he had helped forgot him, because of ungratefulness. Remember, Joseph was ignored and forgotten by the chief butler (Genesis 40: 23). This is an ungrateful society. It is well that we remember that God is our Rewarder (Matthew 6: 4 and

Matthew 16: 27).

He gives some lessons from this (Vv. 16 – 18). He shows how useful a wise man is, "Wisdom is better than strength" (v. 16a); "Wisdom is better than weapons of war" (v. 18a). According to these words, a prudent, wise mind is better than a robust physical body. A wise man can accomplish many things a physically powerful man cannot, and can outwit the man who could overpower him. A wise mind is better than weapons of war, for a wise man will out maneuver those with weapons of war.

He shows how powerful a wise man is (v. 17). That is better translated, "Words of the wise in quiet are heard more than the shout of a chief among fools." A wise man's words, calmly, deliberately spoken, without an attempt to impress with pompous declarations, are powerful. The loud, boisterous shouts of a fool have no power at all. The power of a person's words does not come from the amount, nor volume, but the content. Jesus' words were powerful because they were deliberate and wise, "He does not fight nor shout; He does not raise His voice" (Matthew 12: 19 – The Living Bible).

He shows how a wise man is ignored, "Nevertheless the poor man's wisdom is despised, and his words are not heard" (v. 16b). Just because a man does not have much wealth and successes to his credit, he is despised. Then, he shows how destructive one fool is, "But one sinner destroys much good" (v. 18b). He destroys himself. He wastes the good things God has given him – good sense, good body, good abilities. He destroys his own soul. He destroys others. He can undo all the good that has been done. He can destroy the testimony and reputation of many. One bad person can hinder so many good plans, ideas, and people.

"Wise Sayings and Observations"

Chapter ten seems to be a collection of wise sayings and observations. Yet the general scope is to recommend wisdom to us (Proverbs 8: 1 - 11).

The Admonition to Get Wisdom
(Vv. 1 – 11)

Wisdom will preserve our reputation (Vv. 1 - 3). We must not be guilty of folly (v. 1). The Hebrew expression for "dead flies" is literally "flies of death," or "deadly, poisonous flies." "The flies are poisonous in their bite, or carry infection with them. Such insects corrupt anything that they touch – food, ointment…"[1] "The perfumer's ointment" is the term used by Moses in Exodus 30: 25 in describing the holy anointing which was reserved for special occasions. The "apothecary" (perfumer) is a dealer in spices and perfumes (Exodus 37: 29; 2 Chronicles 16: 14; Nehemiah 3: 8).

"Among the Jew's oil was rendered fragrant by being mixed with precious drugs and was used for many different purposes. With it priests and kings were anointed when they entered upon their office. Guests at the tables of the rich were treated to it as a luxury. It was used medicinally for outward application to the bodies of the sick, and corpses, and the clothes in which they were wrapped were besprinkled before burial. Very great care was needed in the preparation of the material used for such special purposes. Elaborately confected as the ointment was, it was easily spoiled and rendered worthless. It was, accordingly necessary, not only to take great pains in making it, but also in preserving it from contamination when made. If the vase or bottle in which it was put were accidently or carelessly left open, its contents might soon be destroyed. A dead fly would soon corrupt the ointment, and turn it into a pestilent odor. So, says the preacher, a noble and attractive character may be corrupted and destroyed by a little folly. An insignificant looking fault or weakness may outweigh great gifts and attainments."[2]

Just as "dead flies putrefy the perfumer's ointment and cause it to give off a foul odor," so does a little foolishness mar our reputation. Our reputation, which has been achieved with great difficulty and wisdom, may easily be lost by a little folly. We who claim so much godliness must conduct ourselves wisely, and "abstain from all appearances of evil" (1 Thessalonians 5: 22). We will mar the beauty of our wisdom. Just as the poisonous flies so affect the fragrance of the perfumed oil, and cause it to ferment and lose its fragrance, so a little folly mixed with a great deal of wisdom and honor can ruin the reputation of good people. We will destroy the value of our wisdom and godly life. Just as the dealer in ointments cannot sell his corrupted oil, so the person who has committed folly will hinder the authority of his life.

Our wisdom gives us advantages over the fool (v. 2). In those days, the right hand was the place of honor, the left of inferiority. A wise man's sense of understanding is always available to come to his aid when needed. His wisdom is ready always to lead him to what is right, proper and good. His wisdom is ready always to help and guard him (v. 2a). A fool's foolishness will lead him astray in the wrong direction. He is not directed toward righteousness. He has nothing to give him guidance (v. 2b).

Fools constantly expose their foolishness (v. 3). "Even when a fool walks along the way" (v. 3a)... as soon as he sets his foot outside his house and meets other people, he exhibits his folly. If he would stay at home, he would not reveal what a fool he is. His problem is that he doesn't realize that he is a fool, so he mingles with his peers, exhibiting his folly, and has no knowledge that... "he lacks wisdom" (v. 3b). The Hebrew is, "he lacks his mind," or "his understanding is at fault." "And he shows everyone that he is a fool" (v. 3c). His words and actions reveal to everyone that he is a fool. By his irrational behavior, his understanding will fail him at critical times and on important subjects. He will reveal his ignorance, lack of sense, principles, and grace. He will do this in a public manner, because just the way he lives reveals him to be a fool. His foolishness will be seen in an unlimited way, because everyone will come to know him to be a fool.

Wisdom will keep us submitted (Vv. 4 – 11). These verses are here to teach us to be submissive... four ways:

First, we are not to rebel out of disgust (v. 4). The word "spirit" here is equivalent to "anger" (the Hebrew *ruach*, as in Judges 8: 3). If the person in authority over us is angry or displeased with something we have done, or if the person over us in authority rejects and becomes angry at our suggestions and advice, "do not leave your post" (i.e., don't resign, or quit out of anger or disgust). "For conciliation pacifies great offenses." "Conciliation" here means healing, moderation, gentleness, meekness." The truth is that a calm, controlled spirit, one that is not prone to take offense, but patient under trying circumstances, will avoid much sin, heartache, regret, and tragedy. In Proverbs 15: 1, 18 and 25: 15, we are warned that words do kindle anger. Words are spoken that may never be forgotten and forever regretted, thus relationships are strained. Remember: the person who can control his anger (emotions) is much stronger than he who cannot (Proverbs 16: 32). Our example is Christ (1 Peter 2: 21 – 23).

Second, we are not to rebel because we dislike something (Vv. 5 – 7). Verse 5 is speaking of how a ruler, or someone in authority, does something we disagree with ("an error"). Verse 6 is speaking of how one in authority will exalt incompetent people, unworthy favorites to "great dignity" ("great heights"). They are put in eminent positions ("folly" means "fools"), and "the rich," people of nobility and wisdom, are slighted. Verse 7 is speaking of the injustice of fools enjoying power, authority, and wealth while princes (noble, wise, worthy people) are kept in lowly places. Life is filled with injustice and unfairness, as illustrated in these verses, but this is still no reason for us to become embittered and rebellious. Submission endures injustice.

Third, we are not to rebelliously attempt to change things (Vv. 8, 9). Solomon gives us four examples of the harm that is done when such words of wisdom are ignored. 1. "He who digs a pit will fall into it" (v. 8a). The "pit" spoken of here was for the purpose of catching wild animals. If a person was not cautious, he would fall into the very pit he had dug for the animal. The very evil and harm a person plans for another may be reversed, and he will fall into his own trap. This was true with Haman who was hanged on the very gallows he had built for Mordecai (Esther 7: 10). "Plots and conspiracies are often as fatal to the conspirators as to the intended victims."[3]

2. "And whoever breaks through a wall will be bitten by a serpent" (v. 8b). The person who would break through a wall that has been a landmark, can expect the serpent that hides in the hedge to bite him. The "wall" is a hedge, and snakes would hide in the crevices. Thus, the person who removed the hedge (wall) had to keep an eye out for serpents. People in authority are placed there by God, and have His hedge of protection. The person who rebels against and attempts to violently tear down can expect trouble ("will be bitten by a serpent").

3. "He who quarries stones may be hurt by them" (v. 9a). This was the work of the quarryman, as in 1 Kings 5: 17. Such work was exposed to dangers. The wall they are tearing down could fall on them. Solomon is saying that some people are more interested in "tearing down" than mending, demolishing than building up. The very thing (establishment) a person attempts to tear down may fall on them to their own hurt. This speaks of the dangers of such intents.

4. "And he who splits wood may be endangered by it" (v. 9b).The person who cuts up logs, wood, trees, etc., faces the danger of chips flying in his face, the axe or saw injuring him, or a tree falling on him. This is warning those who would destroy time-honored institutions. Their schemes may fly up into their own face, or fall

on them.

Fourth, we are to submit to one another (Vv. 10, 11). These are words of wisdom for both those in authority and those under authority. We are to sharpen the tool we are going to work with (v. 10). The axe is used in cutting wood. If the axe is not kept sharp, the workman will not be prepared for his work, and will only make things more difficult for himself. A fool makes no plans as to how he will prepare himself to fulfill his task. Wisdom teaches a man to prepare himself and carefully plan his endeavor, so he might be effective, for "wisdom brings success." We are to charm the serpent we are to work with (v. 11). Before a snake charmer can work with his snake he must charm him, else he will be bitten. The Bible is saying that we must charm (win to us; gain his favor) the "babbler" (the person who speaks harsh, rough, cruel words) before we can ever work with him. Wisdom will win people, instead of trying to outtalk them.

The Warning of Folly
(Vv. 12 – 20)

In the first eleven verses, Solomon showed to us the merits of wisdom; now he warns us of folly (foolishness).

The words of fools destroy them (Vv. 12 – 14); their words bring them to ruin (v. 12). "The words of a wise man's mouth are gracious" (v. 12a). The wise person's words are not only favorable and pleasing, but they do good to those who hear them. "Gracious words" were spoken by the Lord (Luke 4: 22; Psalm 45: 2). "But the lips of a fool shall swallow him up" (v. 12b). This means more than just "ruin," or "destroy." The fool speaks without forethought, brings shame on himself by what he says, and then must try to withdraw it. His words expose him to reproach and make him look ridiculous. Untimely speech has ruined many a life (Psalm 64: 8). In 1 Kings 2: 23, Adonijah spoke against his own life.

Their words expose their foolishness and corruption, "The words of his mouth begin with foolishness" (v. 13a). The fool speaks according to his nature. As soon as he opens his mouth, he speaks foolishness. 1 Samuel 24: 13, "Wickedness proceeds from the wicked" (Proverbs 15: 2).

Their words injure others, "And the end of his talk is raving madness" (v. 13b). He will talk himself into a state of uncontrolled anger. Before long, he is making accusations that harm others. By the time the fool is finished speaking, he has committed himself to words that are worse than silly, that are presumptuous, frenzied, and indicative of mental and moral depravity.

Their words are vain repetitions (v. 14)... "A fool also multiplies words" (v. 14a). The word for "fool" here is *sakal*, which implies a "dense, confused thinker." He not only speaks foolishly, but he says too much — his words run on endlessly, and he never knows when to stop. He not only says too much, but he goes on and on about things he knows nothing about, talking as though he were an expert on all things. Many who are empty of sense are full of words. "No man knows what is to be" (v. 14b). A fool boasts of what he is going to do, and of his plans for the future, as though they were definite. Because he is a fool he does not realize the foolishness of all this, for no man knows what tomorrow will bring (Proverbs 27:1; James 4:13-17). "And who can tell him what will be after him?" (v. 14c) Not only does he not know what the future may bring, he does not know what things will be like when he is dead and gone! Yet, he speaks as though he does.

By comparing the words of the wise with those of the fool, we discover the following. The wise man's words are few, the fool's endless. The wise man is "swift to hear, but slow to speak" (James 1: 19). The fool hears nothing, learns less, and talks endlessly. The wise man is known by his silence (Proverbs 17: 28; 29: 11). The fool is known by his multitude of words. The wise man's words are gracious; the fool's ruinous. The lips of a wise man are a tree of life (Proverbs 11: 30; 15: 4) and spread knowledge to others (Proverbs 15: 7), while they preserve themselves (Proverbs 14:3). A fool's mouth is his own destruction (Proverbs 17:7) and ruins others. The wise man's words improve as they proceed; the fool's deteriorate as they flow. The more a wise man speaks, the better the words. The more a fool speaks, the worse the words.

The labors of fools have no purpose (v. 15). They weary themselves in their labors, "The labor of fools wearies them" (v. 15a). They labor only for the world and for the body. They exhaust themselves laboring for things that will perish (Isaiah 55: 2). They labor foolishly, "For they do not even know how to go to the city" (v. 15b). The reference to "the city" is referring to their lack of ability to comprehend the plainest thing — they cannot find the huge gate to the entrance to the city. It is right before their eyes but they fail to see it. A fool fails to see the real purpose of labor, which is to store up treasures in heaven and to glorify God. Because they labor for the present (earthly things), they in heaven and to glorify God. Because they labor for the present (earthly things) they become weary. This is one reason why people grow weary in and complain about the work of God. They view it as an earthly obligation and not a divine privilege. They fail to see the gate of the city (i.e., the real eternal purpose for their labors) even though it is right before their eyes. Such a simple thing as finding the entrance to the city a fool cannot do. Likewise, he cannot comprehend the true nature of labor.

Fools will come to ruin (Vv. 16 – 20). The happiness of a land is dependent upon the character of its leaders (Vv. 16, 17). If the leadership is foolish, the people will not be happy (v. 16). "Woe to you, O land, when your king is a child (v. 16a)." The word "child" (Hebrew *naar*) includes any age up to manhood. Here, the "child" is a youthful, inexperienced leader, who does not realize his responsibilities. This is a leader who is without understanding, one who is weak and foolish as a child, fickle, without true direction. "And your princes feast in the morning" (v. 16b). "Feast" here implies feasting and banqueting, beginning the day with sensual enjoyment, instead of honest work and attending to the matters at hand. This implies a person who serves self instead of those whom he is to lead.

If the leadership is wise, the people will be happy (v. 17). "Blessed are you, O land, when your king is the son of nobles" (v. 17a). A man of a noble spirit, who shuns base and unbecoming things because he is a man of character, is a true leader. He is one who puts the interest of the people ahead of his own. "And your princes feast at the proper time" (v. 17b). This is just the opposite of those in verse 16. This kind of person discerns the time, and is responsible to his duties. "For strength and not for drunkenness" (v. 17c)...this speaks of a leader who indulges in times of self-interests and pleasures, solely to gain strength to better perform his tasks. He knows just how much of it he needs, and does not overindulge. He is self-controlled, while a fool is not.

Slothfulness brings evil consequences (v. 18). "Because of laziness, the building decays" (v. 18a). This is the image of a house which falls into ruin for lack of needful repairs. The Bible is saying that a kingdom, country, home, business, marriage, life, etc., decays into ruin because of slothfulness... "and through idleness of hands the house leaks" (v. 18b). The roof lets in the rain. Through laziness of hands, the house will deteriorate. The very imperfect construction of the flat roofs of eastern houses demanded continual attention. A successful life, in all facets, demands constant attention.

Diligence supplies the needs of life (v. 19). "A feast is made for laughter, and wine makes merry" (v. 19a). The leaders spend in revel debauchery the time and energy which they ought to give to the affairs of state. They use God's good gifts of bread and wine as a means of overindulgence and foolish pleasure. They abuse God's gifts to them. "But money answers everything (v. 19b)." The person who will be diligent, not abuse, but use God's gifts, will have ample supply to meet the needs of life.

Disloyalty will be discovered (v. 20). "Do not curse the king even in your thought (v. 20a)." If a person has a slothful leader, the temptation is to criticize them. Here, Solomon warns against it because to harbor evil thoughts may result in speaking against them..."Do not curse the rich, even in your bedroom" (v. 20b). We are not to secretly slander people. What we say in private will be exposed in public (Luke 12: 3). "Walls have ears." "For a bird of the air may carry your voice, and a bird in flight may tell the matter (v. 20c)." We will eventually be found out. Someone will tell the other person of our thoughts and words. This is the same as the expression, "A little bird told me" (Proverbs 6 : 16 - 19).

CHAPTER ELEVEN

"An Exhortation and Admonition"

Exhortation to be Benevolent
(Vv. 1 – 6)

Solomon has previously told us to enjoy what God has blessed us with. Here he tells us to share it.

We are instructed to do so (Vv. 1a, 2a). "Cast your bread upon the waters (v. 1a)." "Cast" means "to send forth." "Bread" means the necessities of life. "Your bread" means that which cost us something. "Upon the waters" means "to give freely;" "send it on a voyage or venture."

"Waters" in Scripture symbolize multitudes of people (Revelation 13: 1). "The bread in the east is made in the form of thin cakes which would float for a time if thrown into a stream. If it be objected that no one would be guilty of such an irrational action as flinging bread into the water, it may be answered that this is just the point aimed at. Do your kindnesses, exert yourself, in the most unlikely quarters, not thinking of gratitude or return, but only of duty."[1] Further, to "cast our bread upon the waters" implies that in many cases we must expect to lose sight of the results of our work; that we must be prepared for disappointment; that at every opportunity "cast our bread," and not always expecting immediate success. Isaiah 32: 20, "Blessed are you that sow beside all waters."

"Give a serving to seven, and also to eight" (v. 2a). Give a "serving." The word for "serving" is that used for the portion of the Levites (Numbers 18: 20). Solomon is saying here not to confine one's offering to the Levites of Judah, but to extend them to the refugees who come from Israel. We are not to give a pittance, but a portion. We are to give a "good measure" (Luke 6: 38). We are to be generous in giving. Give to many, "to seven, and also to eight." We are to give portions of our "bread" to any number of those in need. The message here is unlimited benevolence – the numbers are indefinite. "To seven and also to eight" is a good Hebrew way of saying "to many." Our heavenly Father "gives to all men liberally, and upbraids not," and so must we. "Social economics may, but the Sermon on the Mount does not, condemn indiscriminate or promiscuous giving. One's bread should be cast upon the waters in the same sense that it should be bestowed upon the multitudes, or carried far and wide rather than restricted to a narrow circle."[2] Matthew 5: 42, "Give to him that asks, and from him that would borrow from you, do not turn not away."

We are given the reasons why (Vv. 1b, 2b). We will receive a certain reward, "For you will find it" (v. 1b). It will not be lost, even though by the passing of time and circumstance, it seems to be. As the farmer plants his seed, it seems lost in the ground, but it will eventually sprout and produce "after many days." We will receive a return, though it may be slow, "after many days." "Casting (our) bread upon the waters" will prove to be successful, though it may take time, as the ships of a foreign merchant require much time before they return with the desired profits (James 5: 7; Hebrews 10: 35, 36). The story of true success is the story of patience. Success says, "Work and wait; work diligently intelligently, devoutly, then wait prayerfully and hopefully." Do not be surprised, much less distracted, because the harvest is still far in the future; in due season you will reap, if you faint not. Remember, wheat, the most valuable grain, lies longest in the ground. We have an uncertain opportunity to do so later, "For you do not know what evil will be on the earth" (v. 2b). The time may come when we will not have the means to give of our time, money, talents, self, etc., so we must do it now! (Ephesians 5: 15, 16; Matthew 25: 34 – 40). People are going to be rewarded because they did what they could when they had the opportunity. The time may come when we ourselves will be in need, so we must make friends now (Luke 16: 9; Galatians 6:1).

We are given some common objections to benevolence (Vv. 3 – 6). Some claim that what they have is theirs. They need it for themselves, so why should they share it, "If the clouds are full of rain, they empty themselves upon the earth" (v. 3a). Some may question, "Why should I cast my bread upon the waters?" (i.e., "give to people I do not even know!") 1 Samuel 25: 11 tells us this was the attitude of greedy Nabal. People like this need to look up and see that they would starve from a barren and parched ground if the clouds refused to give rain. Instead of withholding the rain, the clouds, when full, liberally dispel the water. Likewise, as the heavens are bountiful toward mother earth, so must we be toward our brother. Note… "the clouds empty themselves" (i.e., they do not give "a little," but "empty themselves" liberally.) The same liberality we must have toward others.

When the clouds are liberal with their rain, the earth is enriched. The sun then pulls the moisture from the earth back to the clouds, thus, all benefit through giving. The same principles are true in the casting of our bread upon the waters (Luke 6: 38).

Some say that they are not in a position to share as others are, therefore, they will do nothing, "And if a tree falls to the south or the north in the place where the tree falls, there it shall lie" (v. 3b). This is untrue, for "in the place where the tree falls," or happens to be, "there it shall lie," for the benefit of those to whom it belongs. The tree falls in a particular place, for a particular purpose in the providence of God. This is saying that we all must be faithful and be a blessing where God has placed us. The words, "the south, or the north" are emphasizing the particular position is of least importance. What is important is our attitude and opportunity, no matter our position (Matthew 25: 14 – 30, 1 Corinthians 16: 2).

Some say that all the discouraging difficulties in benevolence make it not worth the effort (v. 4). Some have been accused of ulterior motives. Some have seen their gifts misused. Some do not know how their gifts will be used. "He who observes the wind will not sow" (v. 4a). The fact that we do not know what the future holds should not keep us from being diligent and active. The person who must anticipate all results, foresee and provide for all chances, is like a farmer who is always looking to the wind and weather, and misses the time for sowing because of needless caution. "And he who regards the clouds will not reap" (v. 4b). The farmer who anxiously fears every indication of storms, and changes his plans at every change in the sky might easily delay gathering the harvest until his crops are spoiled or the rainy season comes. This is saying that some risks must be taken if we are to do the work of God. We cannot make a certainty of anything. We cannot secure ourselves from failure. We must do our best in faith and the uncertainty of result must never dim our perseverance. Remember... "a watched pot never boils."

Lessons from verse 4: 1. The person who aspires to prosper in his undertakings dismisses all worry; instead of waiting for opportunities, he makes them. According to Proverbs 10: 4, it is "the hand of the diligent" that "makes rich." 2. The person who is always watching the weather, "observing the wind" and "regarding the clouds," will fluctuate at all difficulties and be a failure. In business, as in love and war, the man who hesitates is lost. 3. There is no reason to expect reaping unless sowing has preceded, for "what a man sows that will he also reap." Faithfull toil – thoughtful, patient, persevering toil – will bring a man a successful life. 4. The one who fixes his attention on the difficulties of the task, the lack of his resources, and the examples of past failures, will have his faith crippled, his work brought to a standstill, and his life a disappointment. 5. Something must be endured, and something must be dared, if we are to achieve anything. "If a man wants to sow, he must not mind being assailed by the wind while he is at work; or if he wants to reap, he must not stay indoors because it threatens to rain. We must be ready to endure. We must be prepared to run the risks, if we have any thought of taking rank among the successful workers of our time. God does not give his bounties to those who will only walk the road when it is perfectly smooth and sheltered; nor does he permit us to win triumphs if our heart misgives us at the sight of difficulty or danger. Success is for those, and those only, who can brave wind and rain in the open field of labor, in the wide spheres of usefulness."[3] 6. Everything that is done which is really worth doing is wrought with trouble, difficulty, risk, struggle, disappointment, and with the possibility of failure. It is the contending with adverse "winds" that blow upon us; we have to "put our foot down" firmly on the ground; we have to run the risk of unpleasant "rains" of falling and of failure. This is the price for success.

Some say they do not understand this principle of "giving and receiving," so why should they participate in something they do not understand? (v. 5) We "do not know what is the way of the wind (spirit)" (v. 5a). We do not understand how "life" is conceived in the embryo. We know not "how the bones grow in the womb of her that is with child" (v. 5b). The formation and giving of life has always been a mystery (Job 10: 8, 9; Psalm 139: 15). We do not understand this process. In the same manner, we "know not the works of God who makes everything" (v. 5c). God will keep His promises concerning sowing and reaping though He may not tell us how. God will work and do what He says whether we understand it or not. We are not supposed to always understand... but obey.

Some say they have been benevolent many times, and have yet to be rewarded (v. 6). "In the morning sow your seed (v. 6a)." We are not to let our ignorance of the future, and lack of an understanding of God's dealings, cause us to be apathetical. We are not to allow our opportunities to slip by us, but to be diligent in our calling. "And in the evening do not withhold your hand" (v. 6b). We are not to grow weary in well-doing. We are to labor untiringly throughout the day, no matter what the difficulties and hardships. "For you do not know which will prosper, either this or that, or whether both alike will be good (v. 6c)." We are to be faithful sowers because we never know what seed or how much will bring a harvest (reward) (Galatians 6: 7 – 9).

Admonition to Prepare for Death and Judgment
(Vv. 7 – 10)

These Scriptures tell people of all ages to think of dying, and to get ready for it. Previous portions of Scripture in Ecclesiastes have taught us how to live well; these Scriptures tell us how to die well.

The aged are admonished (Vv. 7, 8). The aged are reminded of the sweetness of life (v. 7), "Truly the light is sweet" (v. 7a). The word "light" can mean "life." This means that the aged are not to be despondent or discouraged over their life, but see both the beauty and the good in the life they have left, "And it is pleasant for the eyes to behold the sun" (v. 7b). To behold the sun is to enjoy life, for light, which is life, is derived from the sun.

The aged are reminded to think of death (v. 8). They are to enjoy their present life, "But if a man lives many years, and rejoices in them all" (v. 8a). It is a man's duty to enjoy life. God has ordained that we do. They are to expect death, "Yet let him remember the days of darkness, for they will be many, all that is coming is vanity

(8b)." There are "days of darkness" coming, the days of our lying in the grave. There will be days when the eyes will see no more; there will be no more light, "For they will be many." The time spent in the grave will be long. "All that is coming is vanity."(v. 8c). Everything that comes after life is over is nothingness; shadow, not substance; a condition in which is absent of all that make life (that is, for our bodies; not our spirit.) The "days of darkness" signify the life of the grave, far from the light of the sun, gloomy, uncheered. However, the thought of such should not depress us, but rouse us to make the best of life, enjoy it, realizing that "the night comes when no man can work (John 9:4)."

"We are reminded of the Egyptian custom … of carrying a figure of a corpse among the guests at a banquet, not in order to damp pleasure, but to give a zest to the enjoyment of the present, and to keep it under proper control. 'Look on this!' it was cried; 'drink, and enjoy thyself; for when thou diest thou shalt be such.'"[4]

The young are admonished (Vv. 9, 10). They are to enjoy their youth, "Rejoice, O young man, in your youth; and let your heart cheer you in the days of youth; walk in the ways of your heart, and in the sight of your eyes" (v. 9a). Youth should take advantage of their youthfulness and enjoy the life around them. They should be adventurous and daring (for God), and not allow life to pass them by.

They are warned of the results of their enjoyments, "But know that for all these God will bring you into judgment" (v. 9b). This reminder will cause a young man to be prudent in his pleasures. This life is not everything, and there is another existence in which a person's life will be tried, justice done, and retribution rewarded.

This judgment will be divine, for the judge will be God (Ecclesiastes 3:17; Psalm 62:12; Isaiah 30:18; Acts 17: 31; Romans 2: 16). It will be individual, because this judgment will be passed, not upon mankind in the mass or upon men in groups, but upon men as individuals. (2 Corinthians 5: 10). Then, it will be certain ("but know") (Hebrews 12: 23; 2 Peter 2:9).

They are cautioned and exhorted (v. 10): Not to defile their minds, "Therefore remove sorrow from your heart" (v. 10a) "Sorrow" means "low spirits, gloom, and discontent." These things are to be put away from their mind by a deliberate act. Not to defile their bodies, "And put away evil from your flesh" (v. 10b). "Evil" means "wickedness." They are to remain morally pure. Use their life properly, "For childhood and youth are vanity" (v. 10c). Their life will soon be gone, too, so they are to live their life right.

"The warning given to young men here was that if one lives carefree, and walks after all the lusts of the heart and the sight of the eyes, he will have to give an account of this, for one is to be judged for everything done in life, whether it be good or bad. In view of this, the youth are advised to remove the things that will cause eventual sorrow of heart, and to put away evil from the flesh so that there will be no pain and remorse in time to come."[5]

"The Whole Duty of Man"

An Exhortation to the Young
(Vv. 1 – 7)

The young are admonished to serve God now, "Remember now your Creator in the days of your youth" (v. 1a). This is Solomon's antidote for the world and its enticing pleasures. They are to "remember" their "Creator." The word "remember" refers to our memory. It means "recollect, reflect, consider, and renew your care for someone." The word "Creator" is the participle of the verb *bara*, which is used in Genesis 1:1, etc., describing God's work.

It is plural in form, like Elohim, the plural being that of majesty or excellence. It speaks of God our Maker (Job 35: 10; Isaiah 54: 5). They are to do this "in the days of (their) youth"... the days when the desire for the world is great.

Note: "Remember your Creator"... Whom? ... "your Creator." Man has a Creator. First, God the Father: 1 Thessalonians 1: 9 says He is "the living and true God." Genesis 1: 1 states He is the Creator (maker) of the universe (Exodus 20: 11; Psalm 124:8; Isaiah 40: 28; Jeremiah 10:16). Genesis 1: 26 says He is the Creator of man (Deuteronomy 4: 32; Psalm 100:3; Acts 17: 25, 26, 28). Second, God the Son (Jesus Christ): 2 Corinthians 4: 4 states He is "the image of God" (Colossians 1: 15). John 1: 1 says He is the Word of God. John 1: 1 – 3 declares He is the Word by whom all things were made, and "by Him were all things created" (Colossians 1:16). Third, God the Holy Spirit: (Genesis 1:2). Man has a knowledge of God. Romans 1: 21, 28 reveals that all men have a knowledge of God, even in their unredeemed state.

However, man can forget God. We discover, in Deuteronomy 6: 12, that this was the sin Israel was guilty of committing. 1 John 4: 8 says this is a basic sin of the world today. Hebrews 3: 12 says this is something believers must guard against. How?... by meditating on His Person. Psalm 10: 4 says God is not in the thoughts of the wicked. Psalm 63: 6 tells us the godly think of God, even in their bed, by remembering His goodness (Psalm 103), and by meditating in His word (Psalm 1).

The reasons for this admonishment (Vv. 1b – 7): Because old age will soon come, "Before the difficult days come and the years draw near when you say, "I have no pleasure in them'"

(v. 1b). Age brings new and challenging difficulties, and limitations that a person has never experienced before.

Because of the calamities of old age (Vv. 2 – 5a), "While the sun and the light, the moon and the stars are not darkened (v. 2a)." The eyesight begins to weaken. The intellectual faculties falter, such as the memory and understanding. "And the clouds do not return after the rain (v. 2b)." Just as one storm cloud passes over and another succeeds it, so does the pains of old age seem to be constant, never ceasing, "In the day when the keepers of the house tremble" (v. 3a). The gradual decay of the body that old age brings is compared to the gradual decaying of an aged house… "And the strong men bow down" (v. 3b). This speaks of the bones - "the strong men"- that become weak and feeble in old age. "When the grinders cease because they are few" (v. 3c), the teeth become few and weak in old age. "And those that look through the windows grow dim" (v. 3d). The eyes are referred to again, "When the doors are shut in the streets (v. 4a)." The speech (mouth, lips) is affected, "And the sound of the grinding is low" (v. 4b). Because the teeth are gone, grinding is not heard when they eat, only the sound of munching and sucking, "When one rises up at the sound of a bird (v. 4c)." No sound sleep anymore. "And all the daughters of music are brought low" (v. 4d)... they lose their ability to sing because of aged vocal cords. "Also they are afraid of height (v. 5a)." They cannot overexert themselves in climbing, high altitudes, etc., because of shortness of breath, "And of terrors in the way; when the almond tree blossoms (v. 5b). "Terrors" speak of their inability to go places by themselves for fear of harm or danger. "The almond tree" speaks of their hair turning white. "The grasshopper is a burden, and desire fails" (v. 5c). Like a "grasshopper" crawls along, so does the aged move slowly when they walk. He loses his desire for any type of physical pleasure.

Because of the changes that death brings (Vv. 5d, e, 6, 7)... death fixes a person in an unchangeable condition, "For man goes to his eternal home (v. 5d)." "His eternal home" is his eternal condition. Death will cause sorrow to his friends, "And the mourners go about the streets" (v. 5e). They had professional mourners in Solomon's day. Here they are used as a type of mourning friends. Death will cause the decay of the body (v. 6). "Remember your Creator before" (v. 6a) is in italics, however it is done so, within the context, to tell the youth to make the best of their time before death cuts them off... "the silver cord is loosed, or the golden bowl is broken (v. 6b)." The "bowl" here is the reservoir of oil in a lamp which supplies nourishment to the flame. When the "bowl" is broken, or damaged, the flame is extinguished. The "cord" is that from which the lamp (bowl) is hung. The thought is that when the cord of life breaks (death), the bowl breaks, and the flame (life) is extinguished. The cord is the "life," and the "bowl" is the body. The body (bowl) decays when its life cord is broken, "Or the pitcher shattered at the fountain, or the wheel broken at the well" (v. 6c). The pitcher here is a deep well, or cistern, with an instrument for drawing water. This instrument consists of a wheel with a rope upon it to which a bucket was attached. If the wheel failed and fell into the well, the bucket was shattered, and no water could be drawn. The motion of the bucket, the winding up and down by which water is drawn from the well, is a type of the movements of the heart and the organs of respiration. If they stop functioning, life is shattered. Death will take a man back from where he came (v. 7). The body will return to the dust from which it came. The spirit will go to face God and give account to Him.

An Admonishment to Consider
What Has Been Written
(Vv. 8 – 12)

Solomon repeats his familiar phrase (v. 8). He did this to show that he had fully demonstrated the vanity of this world. He did this to remind us to remember always that this world is vanity.

Solomon says that what he has written are words of wisdom (Vv. 9 – 12). He says that he was an experienced person, "And moreover, because the preacher" (v. 9a). "And moreover" means "besides that." He is saying, "The world is vanity and besides that I am an experienced person who knows it as well as anyone." He was "the preacher" (*"coheleth"*), one gathered in from his wanderings and gathered home to God from whom he had revolted. Everyone who has been "delivered...from the power of darkness, and ... translated ... into the kingdom of his dear son" (Colossians 1: 13) knows about the vanity of this world.

He was a wise person, "Was wise" (v. 9b). He did not merely possess wisdom, but he made good use of it for the instruction of others. In addition, he taught the people knowledge, "He still taught the people knowledge" (v. 9c). He taught the people the things that had proven to be useful to him. As one who had learned knowledge, he used his wisdom to give the people knowledge. This is a mark of a successful preacher or teacher, one who teaches the people knowledge. In Nehemiah 8:8, Ezra caused the people to understand the reading. Jesus did this (Mark 10: 1). The apostles "taught the people" (Acts 4: 2; 11: 26; 18: 25). According to 1 Timothy 3: 2, 4: 11, 6: 2, and 2 Timothy 2: 2, the pastor is to teach the people knowledge of the word of God.

He says he carefully taught the people, "Yes, he pondered and sought out and set in order many proverbs" (v. 9d). He "pondered" meaning; he "weighed." He carefully examined every fact and argument before he taught it in public. He gave himself to patient study and reverent inquiry. As a shepherd is responsible for the guidance and protection of his flock, the pastor is responsible for diligent, careful, and patient searching for truth to teach his people. "And sought out and set in order many proverbs" means he searched for truth ("sought out"), and organized his truth ("set in order"). Further, he taught a variety of truths ("many proverbs").

He says he taught the people acceptable words, "The Preacher sought to find acceptable words" (v. 10a). "Acceptable words" mean "words of delight," or "comfortable" words. Even though Solomon's thoughts were "higher" than those of his listeners, he spoke his words on their level. A preacher/teacher may be presenting deep, marvelous, and inspirational truth, but what good is it if his listeners cannot understand his words? Solomon spoke "acceptable" words, words that comforted and consoled, and did not offend, just for the sake of offending. 1 Corinthians 14: 3 says ministers should "speak unto men to edification, and exhortation, and comfort" (Proverbs 25: 11). Solomon is saying that ministers should study, not for big words, nor for fine words, but "acceptable words."

He says he taught the truth, "And what was written was upright words of truth" (v. 10b). He wrote things that were sincere ... "upright." He only wrote what he really thought and believed, and what was true objectively. He taught the "truth." Not always what people wanted to hear, but what would direct them! In Isaiah 30: 10, the people did not want the truth, and God is warning them.

He says he taught things that would help people (v. 11). He says the message of the minister should do two things: First, stir the people to action, "The words of the wise are like goads" (v. 11a). The goad was a rod with an iron spike, or sharpened at the end, used to drive oxen (Judges 3: 31; 1 Samuel 13: 21; Acts 9: 5). The "goad" would cause the ox to quicken his pace, speed up, etc. The words of the minister are called "goads," because they are supposed to arouse the people to exertion, action, reflection, and restrain them from wrong and impel them to right. If they hurt and sting, the pain which they inflict is healthful, for good and not for evil. They are "to provoke unto love and good works" (Hebrews 10: 24). Second, stir the people to perseverance, "And the words of scholars are like well-driven nails, given by one Shepherd" (v. 11b). Actually this should read, "The words of the masters of the assemblies are like stakes (nails) which the shepherds drive into the ground when they pitch their tents." "Nails" are instruments of fastening or securing. They keep the cords in their place, and keep the roof over the head of the traveler. Ministers must speak truth that will "ground" the believers in the faith. "Scholars" are "masters of the assemblies," the minister who stands in the worship services to proclaim the word of God. "One Shepherd" is Jehovah. The minister receives his truth from "the Shepherd," Jesus Christ. Ministers are "under shepherds" to Jesus Christ. Additionally, he says the message of the minister should be taught in two ways: 1. By the Scriptures, "The words of the wise" (v. 11a). This is in reference to the writings of the prophets who were "the wise" (2 Timothy 3: 16; 2 Peter 1: 20; 2 Timothy 4: 2). 2. Then, by the speaker, "scholars," the "masters of the assemblies" (v. 11b). He taught what God gave him, "Given by one shepherd" (v. 11c). 1 Corinthians 11: 23, what Paul received from the Lord, he delivered to the people.

He taught things that will guide the people into true happiness (v. 12), "And, further, my son, be admonished by these" (v. 12a), i.e., "...and what is more than these, be warned" by what has been said. Listen now to this additional information... "of making many books there is no end" (v. 12b). As in the eating of food, it is not the quantity which we eat, but what we digest and assimilate that nourishes us, so, in reading, this rule is applicable. Gorging ourselves on secular literature will bring far less mental, intellectual, and spiritual nourishment than a solid diet on the Word of God. Feasting on the Word will keep us from "profane babblings and oppositions of knowledge which is falsely so called" (2 Timothy 6: 20)... "much study is wearisome of the flesh" (v. 12c). "Much study" means "to be eager for." We will weary our brain, and exhaust our strength, by spending long hours in books and other sources that lend no benefit to our spiritual life nor insight into the problems of daily living.

The Conclusion of the Matter

(Vv. 13, 14)

In chapter 2: 3, Solomon said the purpose of this book was to discover "what was good for the sons of men, to do under heaven all the days of their lives" (i.e., what is the true way to happiness and how to achieve it). He admits that he sought for it in every way known to man, and now he has found it. He says, "Let us hear the conclusion of the whole matter" (i.e., the result of this diligent search (Job 28:28).

True relationship... "Fear God and keep His commandments" (v. 13a). Note: "Let us hear the conclusion (end) of the whole matter." This means "everything is heard." The word (*soph*) "end" is printed in the Hebrew text in large characters in order to draw attention to the importance of what is coming. Its significance is rightly estimated. These two verses guard against very possible misconception, and give the author's real and mature conclusion. When this is received, "all that need be said has been uttered."[1]

He says to "fear God." This is the foundation of a godly life. Amid all the confusion in this world, this is the stabilizer. We are to fear God reverently (Deuteronomy 28: 58; Psalm 89: 7; Matthew 10:28; Hebrews 12:28, 29), as a child toward a parent (Psalm 34: 11; Hebrews 12: 9). We are also to "keep His commandments." The commandments for the godly life are found in the Scriptures. Our fear toward God is taught by His commandments. Whenever the fear of God is uppermost in the people's hearts, there will be a respect and obedience to the Word of God (Deuteronomy 11: 18-28; Luke 6: 46, 47; John 14:15).

The importance of relationship... "For this is man's all" (v. 13b). This means "this is every man's duty." This is the reason man was placed in this world, to love and serve God (Ephesians 2: 8 – 10).

The reason for serving God (v. 14)... "For God will bring every work into judgment (v. 14a). Ecclesiastes 11: 9 has already warned that there is a judgment to come in which every person's eternal state will be determined. God Himself will be the judge. Every person's life will be investigated – "every work," "including every secret thing, whether good or evil (v. 14b)." Secret things will be brought to light (Romans 2:16; 14:12). I Corinthians 4:5 says there is nothing that will be hidden on that day.

Conclusion

On November 25, 1895, a cornerstone of ice was laid in Leadville, Colorado. It was the beginning of the largest ice palace ever built in America. In an effort to bolster the town's sagging economy, the citizens staged a winter carnival. On New Year's Day of 1896, the town turned out for the grand opening. The enormous palace measured 450 x 320 feet. The towers that flanked the entrance were 90 feet high. Inside was a 16,000-square-foot skating rink. But by the end of March, the palace was melting away, along with the hopes of Leadville. The thousands of visitors had spent far less than anticipated. Once again, placing ones hope in the temporal proved disappointing.[1]

Solomon has been proven correct time and again, "Vanity of vanities, all is vanity," apart from God. Christ said, "Seek first the kingdom of God and His righteousness, and all these things will be added unto you" (Matthew 6:33). Anything less is nothing more than "chasing soap bubbles."

"Thou has made us for Thyself, O Lord, and our heart is restless until it finds its rest in Thee" (St. Augustine of Hippo).[2]

References

Introduction

1. www.sermonillustrations.com/ (vanity) and Our Daily Bread, July 9, 1994

2. Ibid

Chapter One

1. Dakes Anotated Reference Bible by Finis Jennings Dake, Dake Bible Sales, Inc., P. O. Box 625, Lawrenceville, GA, 30245, 1963, Column 4, p. 498

2. Ibid, Column 1, p. 669

Chapter Two

1. Matthew Henry's Commentary on the Whole Bible, Volume 3, Ecclesiastes, Fleming H. Revell Company, New York, p. 988

2. Dakes Anotated Reference Bible by Finis

Jennings Dake, Dake Bible Sales, Inc., P. O. Box 625, Lawrenceville, GA, 30245, 1963, Column 4, p. 668

3. Ibid, Column 1, p. 669

4. Ibid, Column 1, p. 669

Chapter Five

1. Matthew Henry's Commentary on the Whole Bible, Volume 3, Ecclesiastes, Fleming H. Revell Company, New York, p. 1006

Chapter Six

1. Matthew Henry's Commentary on the Whole Bible, Volume 3, Ecclesiastes, Fleming H. Revell Company, New York, p. 1014

2. Ibid

Chapter Seven

1. The Wesleyan Bible Commentary, Volume
2. Two, Job – Song of Solomon, Ecclesiastes, William E. Eerdmans Publishing Co., Grand Rapids, MI, 1968, p. 622
3. The Pulpit Commentary, Volume 9, Wm. B. Eerdmans Publishing Company, Grand Rapids, MI, p. 199
4. Dakes Anotated Reference Bible by Finis Jennings Dake, Dake Bible Sales, Inc., P. O. Box 625, Lawrenceville, GA, 1963, p. 672

Chapter Eight

1. The Pulpit Commentary, Volume 9, Wm. B. Eerdmans Publishing Co., Grand Rapids, MI, p. 199
2. Ibid, p. 206
3. Ibid, p. 206

Chapter Ten

1. The Pulpit Commentary, Volume 9, Wm. B. Eerdmans Publishing Company, Grand Rapids, MI, p. 249

2. Ibid, p. 206

3. Ibid, p. 206

Chapter Eleven

1. The Pulpit Commentary, Volume 9, Wm. B. Eerdmans Publishing Company, Grand Rapids, MI, p. 275

2. Ibid, p. 281

3. Ibid, p. 288

4. Ibid, pp. 278 – 279

5. Dakes Anotated Reference Bible by Finnis Jennings Dake, Dake Bible Sales, Inc., P. O. Box 625, Lawrenceville, GA, 30245, 1963, p. 675

Chapter Twelve

1. The Pulpit Commentary, Volume 9, Wm. B. Eerdmans Publishing Company, Grand Rapids, MI, p. 306

Conclusion

1. www.sermonillustrations.com/ (vanity) and Today in the Word, August 4, 1991

2. www.goodreads.com/.../425729-thou-hast-made-us-for-thyself-o-lord-and...

Titles by David R. Arnold

Discipleship Manual

Why Do Bad Things Happen to Good People?

When You Don't Know What to Do

60 Seconds January – June

60 Seconds July – December

A Church or a Courthouse

Daniel The Most High Rules in the Affairs of Men

What Will the End Be? The Book of Revelation

Journey of the Patriarchs

Journey of the Patriarchs Workbook

Day of Reckoning

Key of the Day Lock of the Night

Don't Jump Ship

Chasing Soap Bubbles Ecclesiastes

Messiah Prince

All books available in paperback and eBook, on Amazon, Barnes and Noble, and other fine book stores.

To contact for speaking engagements, to place an order, or for free shipping:

davidarnoldministries@gmail.com

Made in the USA
San Bernardino, CA
13 April 2017